W9-AEH-573

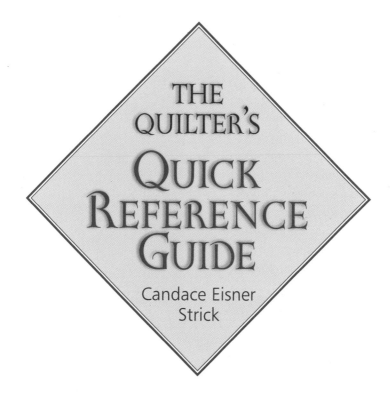

THE QUILTER'S QUICK REFERENCE GUIDE

Candace Eisner Strick

Martingale®
& C O M P A N Y

That Patchwork Place® is an imprint of Martingale & Company®.

The Quilter's Quick Reference Guide
© 2004 by Candace Eisner Strick

Martingale & Company
20205 144th Avenue NE
Woodinville, WA 98072-8478 USA
www.martingale-pub.com

Printed in China
09 08 07 06 05 04   8 7 6 5 4 3 2 1

No part of this product may be reproduced in any form, unless otherwise stated, in which case reproduction is limited to the use of the purchaser. The written instructions, photographs, and designs are intended for the personal, noncommercial use of the retail purchaser and are under federal copyright laws; they are not to be reproduced by any electronic, mechanical, or other means, including informational storage or retrieval systems, for commercial use.

The information in this book is presented in good faith, but no warranty is given nor results guaranteed. Since Martingale & Company has no control over choice of materials or procedures, the company assumes no responsibility for the use of this information.

Library of Congress Cataloging-in-Publication Data

Strick, Candace Eisner.
    The quilter's quick reference guide / Candace Eisner Strick.
        p. cm.
Includes index.
    ISBN 1-56477-532-1
    1. Quilting. 2. Patchwork. I. Title.
    TT835.S7427 2004
    746.46—dc22

CREDITS

President — Nancy J. Martin
CEO — Daniel J. Martin
Publisher — Jane Hamada
Editorial Director — Mary V. Green
Managing Editor — Tina Cook
Technical Editor — Karen Costello Soltys
Copy Editor — Ellen Balstad
Design Director — Stan Green
Illustrator — Robin Strobel
Cover and Text Designer — Shelly Garrison
Photographer — Brent Kane

MISSION STATEMENT
Dedicated to providing quality products
and service to inspire creativity.

Dedication

To all of us who have survived breast cancer, and in loving memory to those who did not—most especially my mother, Sarah Greenspan Eisner. And to the men in my life—Kenneth, Nathaniel, Liam, and Noah.

Acknowledgments

Thank you to the following people:

My quilting buddies Donna McLaughlin, Laurie Mongillo, and Dody Knight—here's to years of fabric buying and friendship.

The people at Martingale & Company who helped me through a very difficult time while I was writing this book—Karen Soltys, Mary Green, Ursula Reikes, and Terry Martin.

My husband, Ken, whose support and love allows me to pursue my dreams and passions.

Quilters everywhere, past and present—your work is inspiration, beauty, and reassurance that the art of quiltmaking will never go out of style.

CONTENTS

INTRODUCTION

My desire to write this book came about as a purely selfish motive. I own many quilt books, but they are mostly books of quilting patterns with a few general technique tips sprinkled here and there. Trying to remember the particular book where I saw a technique explained was too tedious and time-consuming. I wanted to have a quick-reference manual at my fingertips to look up anything that I encountered while making a quilt. I also wanted the book to be totally portable so that I could tote it along in my work bag, and I wanted it to lie flat so that I could do the techniques while glancing at the pages. Thanks to the very talented staff at Martingale & Company, here is such a book!

CHAPTER 1

COLOR AND FABRIC

TO MAKE A QUILT, YOU OBVIOUSLY NEED FABRIC. IN FACT, THE COLORS AND FABRICS ARE USUALLY THE FIRST THINGS THAT DRAW US TO A PARTICULAR QUILT. IT'S WHAT MANY QUILTERS LOVE ABOUT QUILTMAKING—BUYING FABRIC!

There are two schools of thought on how to acquire fabric. The first is to decide upon a quilt design, and then choose and purchase the exact fabrics you wish to use. The second (and most fun) is to build a fabric stash. Buy fabrics that you like when you see them, add them to your collection, and eventually you will have a stash large enough that you can pretty much make a quilt from all the fabrics on hand. When you decide what you want to make, pull out your fabrics and begin to choose. It may end up that you have exactly what you need, or it may end up that you need to purchase more fabric to round things out. With either method, however, there are some general things about fabric that are helpful to know.

Color and Common Terms

Color choice is personal. My philosophy is that if you like it, use it! A color wheel is a tool that shows how various colors relate to other colors. Some quilt designers use a color wheel, and others prefer not to. Either way, it's a good idea to be familiar with it. A color wheel can help you plan a color scheme, such as analogous colors (colors that lie next to each other on the color wheel) that will create a soothing blend, or complementary colors (colors that lie opposite each other on the color wheel) that will give your quilt some punch.

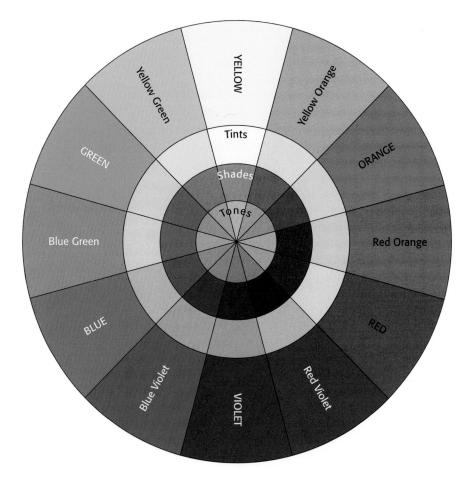

≈ COMMON COLOR TERMS ≈

Primary colors. Red, yellow, and blue—these are the colors from which all others are made.

Secondary colors. A mixture of two primary colors, such as red and yellow combine to make orange.

Intermediate colors. The mixture of one primary and one secondary color, such as blue green or blue violet. These colors are also called tertiary colors.

Hue. Another term for color.

Tint. A color with white added to it to make it lighter.

Tone. A color with gray added to it to make it more subdued.

Shade. A color with black added to it to make it darker.

Intensity. How bright or dull a color appears. This is relative; a color's intensity may change depending on what other color is placed next to it.

Value. The lightness or darkness of a color. Value, too, can be relative. Medium blue will appear dark when placed next to light blue or white, but it will appear light when placed next to navy or black.

Achromatic. Color scheme using only black, white, and grays.

Monochromatic. Color scheme using only one color in various tints, tones, and shades.

Complementary. Color scheme using colors that are directly opposite each other on the color wheel; for example, red and green.

Split complementary. Color scheme using three colors. The colors on either side of the complement are used; for example, blue, red orange, and yellow orange.

Print versus Solid Fabrics

When it comes to fabrics, color is only half the story. Not only do quilters need to decide on what colors they want to use, but they also have to select the style of fabrics. Fabrics are available in solid colors as well as a wide variety of print styles.

Solids

Solid-color fabrics are a single color without any print, markings, or designs. They tend to break up a busy look that can occur when too many prints are combined, and they can be used quite dramatically on their own, as seen in traditional Amish quilts. You should note, however, that solids are also less forgiving than prints when it comes to hiding things like markings or stitching errors.

Prints

Printed fabrics have some sort of design and often contain more than one color, although prints may be made in various shades or tints of just one color. Some prints appear random, while others have a definite pattern or one-way design, such as all flowers facing one direction or vines running from top to bottom but not sideways.

These cats, arches, and bamboo prints are all considered directional.

Prints range in scale from very small to extremely large. Small prints often read as a solid from a distance, but they add an element of texture, and they are great for backgrounds. The patterns of large-scale prints are generally more obvious than those of small-scale prints, and the large-scale prints often contain several colors. Depending on what part of the fabric you cut, a large-scale print can yield pieces that look quite different from one another.

Use a window template to select the portion of a large-scale print you want to use.

For more on specific types of prints, see the individual categories below and on the following pages.

Dots

Dots are prints with an actual dot or other very small motif printed onto a solid-color background. Sometimes called conversation prints, these designs may be complex up close, such as kittens, horseshoes, or other common objects, but from a distance they appear as dots. Because it's hard for the eye to focus on the actual motif, it's a good idea to limit the number of these prints used in a single quilt.

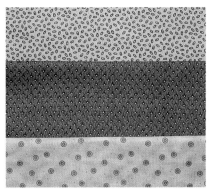

Dots can be close together or not, arranged in a regular pattern or scattered.

Florals

Floral motifs are perhaps the most common type of print available to quiltmakers. Florals range in size from small to large, and they can feature one color or many colors.

Floral patterns may be arranged formally or scattered irregularly as plants in a cottage garden.

Curved-Line Prints

Curved-line prints are fabrics with wavy designs. They can feature meandering vines or a nonspecific print that curves and meanders. They add wonderful interest to the straight, geometric lines of most pieced quilts.

Notice that curved-line prints are directional.

Theme Prints

In addition to the various types of prints already mentioned, many quilters like to work with what is commonly called a theme print. As the term suggests, this fabric sets the tone or theme for the remaining fabric choices. The prints can be floral, pictorial, geometric, or whatever you like. They are used as the basis for selecting additional fabrics for the quilt.

Here are a few of the many choices available as theme fabrics:

Batiks: These fabrics are printed in Indonesia, and the designs are often hand stamped using a wooden chop. Batiks are tightly woven fabrics and come in an unbelievable assortment of colors, both bright and subdued, and in both near solids and prints.

Toile: The traditional French print of idyllic country life has been expanded to include all kinds of designs. Toiles are generally two-color fabrics.

Nostalgic prints: Evoking the placid pace of life in the 1950s, some of these fabrics show Mom in the kitchen, and Dick and Jane at play.

Reproduction prints: Fabric designs from many bygone eras, such as the Civil War, the turn of the twentieth century, and the 1930s and 1940s, are now available to quilters.

Vintage florals: Slightly faded look-ing, soft, and serene, vintage florals are very popular.

Animals: Teddy bears, cats, rabbits, wild animals—the list can go on and on. You can select fabric that features your favorite animal and make a quilt with it.

The theme prints shown here include a holiday pictorial (top), a large-scale floral (center), and a geometric print (bottom).

Stripes

Stripes have bands of design that usually run parallel to the selvage of the fabric. They yield interesting designs when cut into patchwork pieces. And they are excellent for borders, especially when the corners are mitered, and for bias binding.

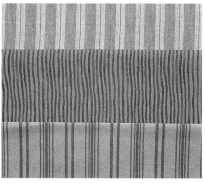

Stripes may be woven into the fabric or printed on top as in the center example.

Plaids

Plaids can be either woven (the same on both sides of the fabric) or printed (with a clear right and wrong side of fabric). The distin-guishing characteristic of plaids is that they have lines that run both parallel and perpendicular to the selvage.

Printed plaids can be tricky to work with, because the lines are not always printed exactly on the straight of grain. They may require careful cutting, sometimes off grain, in order for the lines to look straight in the project. Or, if you want to give a quilt a homespun look, you can take advantage of off-grain lines and leave them as is.

An assortment of printed and woven plaids shows that plaids can be complex or quite simple.

Tone-on-Tones

Tone-on-tone fabrics use several different tones of one color in their patterns. These fabrics are subtle but add more interest and texture than can be achieved with a solid fabric.

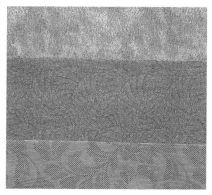

Tone-on-tone prints are a good way to add visual texture to a quilt.

Selecting Fabrics

Whether you plan to use what you already own or you are buying fabric for a specific project, you will need a working assortment of fabric. Don't be afraid to take lots of choices off the shelf—whether in your sewing room or at the quilt shop—as you plan your next quilt. Here are some general guidelines to follow when choosing fabrics:

- Variety, as they say, is the spice of life. The same goes for quilts. Make sure you use both small- and large-scale prints.
- Consider solids; used with lots of prints, they can give your eye a place to rest. Remember that sometimes a tiny print or a tone-on-tone print can work like a solid.
- It is good to have a few "ugly" prints to throw in. Too many gorgeous, bright, and splashy prints can become boring or make the quilt look muddled. Putting a duller fabric next to a bright one makes for good contrast.
- Use a wide variety of both darks and lights to achieve contrast in your quilt.
- Too many fabrics of the same color can be monotonous. Don't be afraid to mix in something that you think doesn't go.
- If you are making the quilt to coordinate with a certain decor, try to choose fabrics that aren't already part of the color scheme.

By making every fabric choice exactly match the room's color scheme, the quilt is apt to blend in instead of stand out.

- If you are buying fabrics to collect, try to have a good representation of every color on the color wheel. We tend to buy just our favorite colors, but for a quilt to be really exciting or for us to expand our expertise at using color, we need to use those colors that are not our favorites. In small doses, they may be exactly what your next quilt needs!

Determining How Much Fabric to Buy

If you are following a particular pattern, it will specify the yardage you need. If you are buying to expand your stash or to make something yet to be determined, here are a few general guidelines to help you decide how much of a particular fabric to buy.

- In choosing coordinating fabrics for a quilt, aim for about three to seven different fabrics.
- The more pieces the quilt has, the more fabric you will need. Remember, each piece has a ¼" seam allowance on all sides. This adds up quite quickly in terms of extra fabric.
- Fat quarters (18" x 22") are convenient to buy and are great for small projects or scrap quilts. For larger quilts, think about purchasing ½-yard cuts or more—especially if you really love a particular fabric.

⚋ IF YOU RUN OUT OF FABRIC ⚋

If you run out of a fabric while making a quilt, don't panic; view it as a wonderful opportunity. You can take the partially completed quilt, or a single block, to the store to audition a new fabric. I haven't taken a poll on this, but I would bet that most quilters experience this situation, where they start a project and then end up having to purchase additional fabric. The reasons for needing more fabric can vary, from changing one's mind about the size of the quilt in progress to simply running out of a fabric or wishing to add more fabrics to the original idea.

Sometimes running out of fabric and not being able to get more of the original can seem like a challenge. I like to look at it as an opportunity to jump-start my creativity. By making a fabric substitution or altering your original design, you might change the whole direction you anticipated, and that can be an exciting thing!

- Buy background fabrics in quantities of about two to four yards, depending on whether you want to make a wall quilt, a lap quilt, or a bed quilt.
- Backing fabric, of course, depends on the size of the quilt, so you may want to hold off buying it until you need it. Five to six yards is generally sufficient for a twin- or full-size quilt, while a queen- or king-size quilt can require eight to ten yards. Or, consider piecing a scrappy backing (using more than one fabric) if your goal is to save money and reduce your fabric stash.
- It takes about one-and-a-half to two times more fabric for a quilt top as for a quilt back.

Deciding to Prewash Fabric—or Not

Whether or not you prewash your quilting fabrics is a personal preference. Some quilters like unwashed fabric for the crisp feel that comes from the sizing put on the fabric during the manufacturing process. Others are concerned that the colors might bleed or that the fabric will shrink when a quilt is eventually washed, and they want to prevent this from happening by washing the fabric before cutting and sewing it.

Effects of Prewashing Fabric

- Removes the sizing used in the manufacturing process, giving it a softer hand
- Removes any excess dye, making the colors less prone to run when the entire quilt is washed for the first time
- May shrink fabric

Effects of Not Prewashing Fabric

- Retains a crisp hand that many quilters prefer
- May shrink later, when the finished quilt is washed, giving it an instant antiqued look

How to Prewash Fabric

Sort fabric colors by light and dark, and wash in two separate batches. I like to use hot water with a small amount of detergent or none at all. Then I dry the fabric on high heat and press it when it comes out of the dryer. I prefer using high heat because I figure this will be the harshest treatment my quilt will ever endure. But if you prefer, you can wash the fabrics in warm water and dry on medium heat.

CHAPTER 2

TOOLS OF THE TRADE

YOU CAN MAKE A QUILT WITH PRECIOUS FEW HIGH-TECH TOOLS. THE ONLY REAL NECESSITIES ARE SCISSORS, THREAD, AND NEEDLES, SINCE THESE WERE OBVIOUSLY THE ONLY TOOLS OUR ANCESTORS HAD AVAILABLE WHEN MAKING THEIR QUILTS. I'M QUITE SURE, THOUGH, THAT THEY WOULD BE THRILLED WITH THE LABOR-SAVING GADGETS WE HAVE AT OUR DISPOSAL. THE BASIC TOOLS AND SUPPLIES, AS WELL AS SOME NOT-NECESSARY-BUT-NICE-TO-HAVE OPTIONS, ARE DESCRIBED BELOW.

Sewing machine. All kinds of models are available, from treadle to electronic to computerized. For basic piecing, you need a smooth-running machine that makes a nice, even straight stitch. One trick to getting a terrific straight stitch on a machine designed to do zigzag and other decorative stitches is to replace the throat plate that has a wide needle opening with one that has only a small hole opening. These throat plates are made specifically for straight stitching and will prevent your fabric from being pulled into the opening. If you're

Whether high-tech or old-fashioned, all you need for patchwork is a machine that sews a smooth, straight stitch.

not happy with your machine's straight stitch, you don't need to trade it in; for the price of a throat plate, you can improve it.

If you want to machine appliqué, you'll need a machine that does zigzag or blind stitch. For machine quilting, you'll need a walking foot (some machines have them built in) and a darning foot for stitching through the layers.

Rotary cutter. This device has a razor-sharp circular blade attached to a handle, and it allows you to cut through several thicknesses of fabric in one stroke. Rotary cutters are available in a variety of metric sizes: 28, 45, 60, and 65 mm. For general use, the 45-mm cutter is the most common choice. The smaller rotary cutters are good for cutting curved pieces, while the larger ones work well for heavy-duty cutting, like flannel or home decorating fabrics. In addition to size, consider the type of handle that works best for you when selecting a rotary cutter: straight or curved. Rotary cutters can be used with either your right or left hand.

Cutting mats and rulers. A self-healing mat is used in conjunction with a rotary cutter to protect your table from blade damage. Mats are available in different sizes, some with grid lines printed on them and some without grid lines. The lines on a cutting mat aren't as accurate as those on a ruler, and with repeated use the lines can wear off. You may want to learn to cut on the plain side of your mat and only use your ruler for measuring. Some quilters find that using a mat without the lines is less distracting.

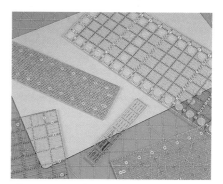

Cutting mats have a plain and printed side. The plain sides are typically green or gray, and create less distraction for viewing the ruler lines. Rulers also vary in color; look for those that are easiest for you to read accurately.

Choose a rotary cutter with a handle style that fits comfortably in your hand.

To measure and cut your fabric, you'll need clear acrylic rulers specifically designed for use with a rotary cutter. You'll find them in a huge variety of shapes and sizes. The size I use almost exclusively measures 6" x 24", although a large square ruler can be handy for cutting setting squares and appliqué blocks or squaring up pieced blocks. You may also want a shorter ruler to toss in your tote bag for trips to classes or quilting retreats.

Scissors. While much of your cutting will be done with a rotary cutter, every quiltmaker needs scissors. From cutting templates and appliqué shapes to snipping threads, what would we do without scissors? Keep a small pair of embroidery scissors or thread snips by your sewing machine for cutting threads. Keep fabric scissors out of reach of your family members so that they don't use them to cut sandpaper. Your scissors will stay sharp and be readily available when you need them.

Seam ripper. Another handy cutting tool that no quilter should be without is a seam ripper. (I own about five of them!) As much as we hate to admit it, we all need to unsew at some time or another.

Pins. Very thin straight pins, called silk pins, are good for holding pieces of fabric together for accurate stitching. If you machine quilt, you'll also need safety pins for basting together the quilt layers.

Needles. It's good to keep a supply of machine and hand-sewing needles on hand. Machine needles should be changed after every eight hours or so of sewing. They become dull or nicked, and they can make pulls in your fabric. Sizes 11/75 or 12/80 are good for piecing; size 14/90 is good for machine quilting. For machine appliqué, choose machine embroidery needles, which have a longer scarf in the needle to allow the thread to flow easily in and out of the layers.

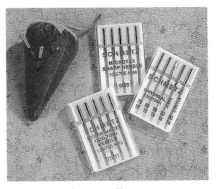

Sewing-machine needles come in a wide variety of styles and sizes, so read the labels carefully when making your selection.

Thread. Look for long-staple cotton thread, which can be found at any quality quilting or sewing store. Avoid bargain brands. They create a lot more lint, requiring more frequent machine cleaning. Gray or tan are good color choices to blend with a variety of patchwork colors.

Bobbins. Keep multiple bobbins on hand. While you're filling one, you might as well fill a backup. That way, when you run out of thread, you have one ready to pop in your machine and you can keep right on sewing.

Iron. A good iron is essential for neat and accurate work. I like to use steam, but many quilters prefer to use dry heat. Nowadays, many irons have an automatic shut-off feature. Some quilters see this as handy; others see it as a curse! If you don't want to have to continually restart your iron every 10 minutes or so, you might want to look for an iron without this built-in feature.

Ironing board. Make sure your ironing surface is at a good height for you. Some can be adjusted to a variety of heights. If you're tall, you may want to set up your own system so that you don't have to hunch over while pressing fabric. Wrapping a hollow-core door with batting and canvas and positioning it across file cabinets may be a good alternative to a wedge-shaped ironing board, as it will give you extra pressing space for larger pieces of fabric.

Lighting. Good lighting is essential in a sewing room, especially if you find that most of your quilting gets done in the evening hours. A single overhead light isn't always enough to help you see what you're doing and to prevent eyestrain. Portable lamps for cutting and sewing tables are a good option. You can use tabletop or clamp-on models, as well as floor lamps. Look for true-color or daylight bulbs, which are particularly helpful for matching fabrics because they more closely represent actual daylight conditions.

≈ GADGETS GALORE ≈

When it comes to gadgets, hardware stores have nothing on quilt shops! Many quilters love nifty gadgets, while others prefer just the basics. Here are some gadgets you may want to add to your sewing room to save you time or frustration.

The Angler. If you like to make triangle squares or bias squares by layering two squares and sewing ¼" away from the diagonal center, then this tool can save you time. It's a clear plastic sheet that you tape onto the throat of your sewing machine. Simply guide the fabrics along the appropriate markings on the Angler and there is no need to mark either the diagonal center or the sewing lines on your squares.

Invisi-Grip. What a clever invention! Invisi-Grip, made by Omnigrid, is a clear plastic film that can be cut to any size and positioned on the back of rotary-cutting rulers. It prevents rulers from easily slipping while you're cutting fabric, yet it's still easy to reposition the ruler when you want. And because it's clear, it doesn't hinder seeing through the ruler to your fabric. Because Invisi-Grip works with static cling, it can easily be removed and used on another ruler.

Needle threader. Many models are available, but if you have a hard time threading tiny-eyed needles, the Desk Needle Threader by Clover is a true wonder. You just position the needle in the box, lay the thread over the groove in the box, and press the button. Voilà! Even most tiny-eyed hand-quilting and straw needles can be threaded with this item.

Reducing glass. When planning a quilt, it's helpful to step back and view your project from a distance to see how the color placement is working. If you work in a small space, however, stepping back isn't always an option, but using a reducing glass is. Use this small gadget to view your project and you'll see it as though you were standing 10 feet away. If you live in a two-story dwelling, you can also try this: Place the quilt on the first floor, and then view the quilt from the vantage point of the staircase.

Ruby Beholder®. When held over a fabric, this red Plexiglas tool takes away the color and leaves you looking only at value (dark, medium, light). If you find color planning a challenge, this tool may be for you. You can also find green value finders that are good for viewing warm colors—red, orange, yellow, and violet. Use the red one for cool colors—blues and greens.

Ruler rack. A simple wooden rack with notched-in grooves holds an assortment of rulers. It will help you clear up the clutter on your cutting table and put all your rulers within easy reach.

A ruler rack will help keep your cutting table organized, while using Invisi-Grip on your rulers will make cutting a breeze. Clover's needle threader makes quick work of threading needles of all sizes, and a Ruby Beholder will help you plan your color selections.

CHAPTER 3

ROTARY-CUTTING TECHNIQUES

QUILT PIECES CAN BE CUT WITH A HIGH-QUALITY, SHARP PAIR OF SCISSORS. AFTER ALL, THIS IS THE WAY OUR ANCESTORS CUT QUILT PIECES. HOWEVER, I'M QUITE SURE THAT IF THEY SAW THE ROTARY-CUTTING METHODS THAT ARE POPULAR TODAY, THEY WOULD QUICKLY CONVERT. IN THIS CHAPTER, WE'LL REVIEW SOME OF THE BASICS OF ROTARY CUTTING, ALONG WITH THE BEST WAYS TO CUT PARTICULAR SHAPES. BUT FIRST, LET'S REVIEW SOME SAFETY TIPS FOR ROTARY CUTTERS.

Safety First!

Rotary cutters have virtually revolutionized the world of quiltmaking. Most quilters wouldn't give them up, but they are very sharp and can be dangerous if not handled properly.

- Keep the blade in the closed position when not in use; this means *every time you put the cutter down*—even of it's just to reposition the fabric or ruler. In addition to being a safety precaution, it protects the blade from possible nicks.

- Hold the cutter correctly. Let the cutter rest in the palm of your hand, extend your index finger forward (it will help balance the cutter when you use it), and wrap your other three fingers around the opposite side of the handle from your thumb.

- Always cut away from your body. Besides being safer, you have greater strength in pushing than in pulling.

- Keep all fingers of your noncutting hand firmly on the ruler and well out of the way of the cutter.

• Change the blade as soon as it feels dull or if it has a nick or burr that makes it skip threads. If you're having to use more pressure to cut through your fabric layers, it's time to change the blade. Otherwise, you'll be putting undue stress and strain on your wrist, arm, and shoulder. And you'll be tempted to cut back and forth to trim stray threads, which is definitely not a good idea.

Always cut away from yourself and keep fingers out of the way!

Fabric Grain

Before cutting any fabric, make sure it is pressed and wrinkle free. And you should straighten the grain of the fabric so that your pieces will be cut on grain. Why is this important? Edges cut on grain have the least amount of stretch, making them easier to sew and less likely to stretch out of shape in the finished quilt. When pieces are cut off grain, you'll start to notice a bit of stretchiness to them, even if they aren't cut on the true bias (a 45° angle from the straight grain).

Grain line refers to the straight lines of threads from which the fabric is woven. The warp threads are the lengthwise threads, and these have the least amount of stretch or give. The weft threads are the horizontal threads (selvage to selvage). These have a little bit of give, but they are nothing like fabric that is cut on the bias. The selvage runs the length of the fabric and is woven much more tightly than the rest of the fabric. Its purpose is to hold the fabric in place on the loom while it is being woven. Never use the selvage in your quilt patches—not even in the seam allowances.

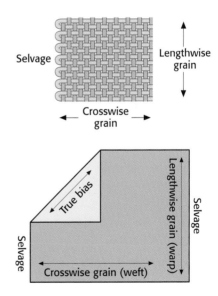

23

Straightening the Grain

Before cutting your patches, make sure the fabric is on grain and not twisted or pulled out of shape. When you fold the fabric in half so that the two selvage edges meet, the cut ends of the fabric may not align. That's okay, because the fabric may have been cut crookedly. But check to be sure that the weft or crosswise threads are folded evenly and not crooked.

To check the crosswise grain, make a crosswise snip near the end of the fabric at one selvage, and then tear across to the other selvage. This will automatically make your crosswise grain true. (It may also cost you several inches of fabric if it was not originally cut straight.) When the fabric is folded with the selvage edges aligned, the torn edge of the fabric should also be aligned. If the torn edges still do not meet, you may need to tug your fabric gently along the bias (diagonally) to realign the threads. When you've straightened the fabric, refold it and press. If you already have a crease pressed along the original fold line, you may need to dampen the fabric and re-press it.

Cutting on Grain

As rule of thumb, cut each piece with as many sides on grain as possible. The goal of the pieced block is to have all four outer edges on the straight grain because this gives your blocks the most stability. Some shapes, like strips, squares, and rectangles, are cut with all edges on the straight of grain. But other shapes, like triangles, diamonds, and curved pieces, will always have one or more sides on the bias. The location of those pieces within the quilt blocks determines which edges should be cut on grain and which should have the bias stretch.

All Edges Cut on Grain

Some Edges Cut on Bias

Snowball Block

Note that all outer edges of the block are on the straight of grain; bias edges are contained within the block.

If a quilt is to be hung on a wall, cut all the borders along the lengthwise grain of the fabric. The lengthwise strips will have the most strength and stability to withstand the weight of the quilt. This is also true with the backing fabric.

If the quilt is to lie on a bed, it makes no difference if you cut the borders and backing on the crosswise or lengthwise grain, since the bed will support the weight of the quilt. The only time the grain of the border fabric would be a concern is if your fabric is directional, such as a stripe or a print with a clear top and bottom to the design. Then you may want all the borders to be cut so that the stripe or print appears to be going in the same direction.

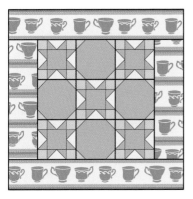

Directional Border Print

✒ PLANNING ✒ FOR BIAS

If your quilt pattern calls for lots of pieces that have bias edges, try to choose a tightly woven fabric, such as a batik, since that will have less stretch in the bias than a loosely woven fabric, such as a homespun.

Cutting Strips Accurately

To start, straighten the grain and fold the fabric with selvage edges aligned as described in "Straightening the Grain" on page 24. If desired, you can fold the fabric again, matching the folded edge with the selvages. However, be aware that the more layers you cut at one time, the less accurate your cutting is apt to be. If the folds along each edge of the fabric are not perfectly parallel to one another, the strips you cut will not be completely straight and on grain. To assure that your strips are entirely straight, follow the steps below.

1. Place a 6" x 12" or 6" x 24" ruler on the fabric so that one of the crosswise lines is aligned with the fold closest to you. Make sure that a little bit of each layer of your fabric extends beyond the side of the ruler that you'll be cutting along.
2. Trim off the narrow strip of fabric that extends beyond your ruler to straighten the edge of the fabric.
3. Place the ruler on the fabric and measure in from the cut edge the distance that you want your strip to be. If you want a 2"-wide strip, align the 2" marking line along the cut edge of the

fabric. One of the horizontal lines on the ruler should still be perfectly aligned with the folded edge of the fabric. If it's not, your strip won't be totally straight.

4. If you're ambidextrous, you can now cut along the opposite edge of the ruler to cut your strip. If not, you need to walk to the opposite side of your cutting table, or turn the mat (taking care not to move the fabric), so that you can cut with your dominant hand. Cut along the ruler and open up the strip. Check to make sure that it is straight and not bent into a V shape at the fold. If the strip is not straight, refold and trim your fabric so that the fold is parallel to the selvage edge.

V Shape at Fold

Fabric folded and cut properly.

5. Continue cutting strips in this manner, sliding your ruler the distance needed to cut the appropriate strip width. Because it's nearly impossible to fold fabric perfectly, check to make sure the folded edge is still perpendicular to your cut edge after every two or three cuts. If it gets off (a common occurrence), align one of the horizontal lines of the ruler with the folded edge and trim up the cut edge of the fabric. Now you're ready to continue cutting strips. Taking the time to straighten the fabric as needed will prevent you from having strips that are bent in the center.

∼ CUTTING ∼ ON THE DOUBLE

If you decide to cut by folding your fabric and then folding it again (in other words, four layers at a time), you'll have two folded edges to deal with. When you are lining up your ruler to make your straightening cut, make sure the two folded edges are exactly parallel to one another. If you line up one fold with the 1" line on the ruler, but the other fold is at a bit of a diagonal to a horizontal line on the ruler, your fabric strips won't be straight. Save yourself some aggravation and refold the fabric before you even make the first cut.

Cutting Shapes from Strips

If you're planning to cut shapes from the strips, leave the strips folded. When cutting the shapes, you'll get two (or four if you cut with a double fold) from each cut you make.

Squares

Cut strips that are ½" wider than the finished size of your squares to account for seam allowances. Trim off the end of the strip to remove the selvage and to square up the ends of the strip. Then measure in the same distance as the width of the strip. Make sure the ruler is aligned along the top of the strip and the cut end of the strip. Cut as many squares as the length of the strip allows, or cut as many as you need. The piece you have left at the end will be the fold. If you open this piece, there may be enough for another square, but only cut a square from it if it's straight and not V-shaped.

Rectangles

As with squares, start with a strip that is ½" wider than the finished width of your rectangle. Square up the end of the strip. Then cut the desired length, again accounting for ½" seam allowances. Make sure the horizontal and vertical lines of the ruler align on the strip.

Half-Square Triangles

Cut strips and then squares that are ⅞" larger than the finished size of your triangles. Cut each square in half diagonally, from one corner to the opposite corner, to yield two triangles per square. If your plan is to mix up the colors and sew the triangles together in pairs to make triangle squares, you may want to try the shortcut method on page 28.

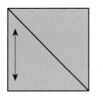 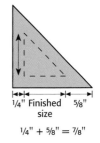

¼" Finished   ⅝"
size

¼" + ⅝" = ⅞"

~~ TRIANGLE-SQUARE SHORTCUT ~~

With this method, you start with squares, sew them together on the diagonal, and then trim them apart to yield two identical triangle squares. In this case, start with squares that are the size of your desired finished triangle squares, plus ⅞" for seam allowances.

1. Cut two contrasting squares to the size needed. On the wrong side of the lighter of the two squares, mark a diagonal line from one corner to the opposite corner with a pencil and ruler.

2. Layer the squares right sides together and stitch ¼" from each side of the line. Cut the squares apart on the diagonal line with a rotary cutter and ruler. Press the seams toward the darker fabric; yield two triangle squares.

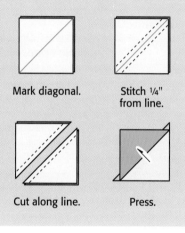

Mark diagonal.   Stitch ¼" from line.

Cut along line.   Press.

Quarter-Square Triangles

Quarter-square triangles are one quarter of a square. The way they are cut puts the straight grain of the fabric along the longest edge of the triangle, instead of on the two short edges as with half-square triangles. To account for seam allowances on this shape, cut the initial strip 1¼" wider than the finished length of the base of the triangle. Cut the strip into squares, and then cut the squares in half diagonally in both directions to yield four triangles per square.

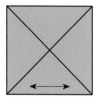

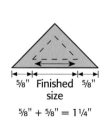

⅝" Finished ⅝"
size

⅝" + ⅝" = 1¼"

QUARTER-SQUARE SHORTCUT

Quarter-square triangles are used for setting triangles (see page 80), but quite often they are used to make quarter-square triangle units that are actually Hourglass blocks. If you need to make setting triangles, cut them as described, opposite. However, if you plan to sew the individual triangles back together to make a colorful pieced square, you can use this shortcut method where you sew first, and then cut.

1. Starting with squares that are 1¼" larger than your desired finished size unit, make two triangle squares as described in "Triangle-Square Shortcut," opposite. If you want your finished quarter-square-triangle unit to have just two colors, make two identical triangle squares. If you want to have scrappier-looking quarter-square-triangle units, you can use two different triangle squares (four different fabrics total).

2. On the wrong side of one of the triangle squares, draw a diagonal line from corner to corner that is perpendicular to the existing seam line. Then layer the two triangle squares right sides together, seam lines aligned. Make sure that you place the triangle squares so that the light fabric of one is on top of the dark fabric of the other one.

3. Sew ¼" from each side of the drawn line. Cut the squares apart on the diagonal line using a rotary cutter and ruler. Press the seams to one side to yield two quarter-square-triangle units.

Mark diagonal.

Stitch ¼" from line.

Cut along line.

Press.

Cutting Shapes with Templates

Some patchwork shapes are more complex than squares and triangles, but if they have straight edges, you can use your rotary cutter and ruler in conjunction with a template to cut these pieces. Measure the width of the template (including seam allowances), taking into consideration how you want to position the shape along the grain line. Cut a strip that width.

Then place the template on the fabric, position the ruler along the edge of the template, and cut. Repeat for other edges of the shape. Often the first cut shape will provide a clean-cut edge where you can place the template for the next cut. If that's not the case, position the template beyond the irregular ends and cut as before.

For shapes with some curved edges, such as those for Drunkard's Path blocks, you can cut along all straight edges with a rotary cutter, and then cut the curved portion by hand with scissors.

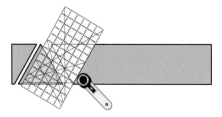

Place ruler over template and cut.

 BLUNT-CUT
POINTS

Long points on the ends of some shapes can make sewing hard because it's not always easy to tell how to line them up with other patches. Additionally, the long ends sometimes get crumpled up in the feed dogs. To eliminate these problems, use your rotary cutter and ruler to blunt cut the points at a 90° angle as shown.

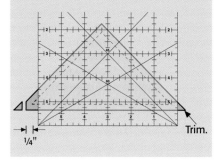

Trim.

1/4"

CHAPTER 4

SEWING PIECES

MOST QUILTERS WOULD PROBABLY AGREE THAT SEWING IS THE FUN PART OF THE QUILTING PROCESS. PREWASHING, PRESSING, AND CUTTING FABRIC ARE JUST THE THINGS WE NEED TO DO TO GET READY FOR THE BUSINESS OF SEWING A QUILT, ALTHOUGH I ADMIT THAT I ENJOY THESE STEPS BECAUSE THEY GET ME ACQUAINTED WITH THE FABRIC AND HELP ME WITH THE DESIGN PROCESS.

Basics for Good Machine Sewing

Successful quiltmaking greatly depends on your preparation. Make sure your machine is oiled and running smoothly. Use the appropriate thread and needles, and check the settings on your machine for stitch length and seam allowance.

Thread

Most quilters like for the fiber content of their fabric and thread to match. So, if you're using 100%-cotton fabric, choose 100%-cotton thread too. Size 50/3 is a good choice. The first number, 50, refers to the diameter of the thread. The higher the number, the thinner the thread. The second number, 3, refers to the number of plies that are twisted together to make up the thread. The higher the number, the more plies the thread has and thus the stronger it is.

Needles

A needle size of 75/11 or 80/12 is a good choice for medium-weight cotton fabric. The first number is the European size; the second number is the American size. The higher the number, the bigger the needle. Note that this is only true for machine needles, not hand-sewing needles.

In addition to different sizes, machine needles come in a variety of styles for different sewing needs.

Choose needles that are labeled "universal," which means the point does not pierce the individual yarns of the fabric but rather goes between the threads. More specifically, you can choose needles labeled "quilting," but make sure to use the appropriate size. They are often packaged with both 75/11 and larger 90/14 needles in the same box. The larger needles are suitable for machine quilting through batting, but not for piecing. See page 131 for a needle-size chart.

Stitch Length

Some sewing machines have a stitch-length guide that is measured in millimeters, while others use stitches per inch. A stitch length of 12 to14 stitches per inch is ideal for piecing, which translates to the setting of 1.75 to 2.0 on metric machines. See page 131 for a stitch-length comparison chart.

Seam-Allowance Width

The universal standard for patchwork seam allowances is ¼". Even if your sewing machine has a ¼" mark on the throat plate or has a ¼"-wide patchwork foot, you need to test the seam allowance to make sure that it's accurate. You can sew seams that are ¼" wide, but after accounting for the thread width and pressing, your patchwork may come up short. Here's an easy way to test your results.

1. Place a rotary-cutting ruler (one with ¼" increment markings) under the presser foot and lower the needle so that it is just above the ruler. The ruler should be positioned so that the ¼" line is just a hair to the left of the needle and the edge of the ruler is ¼" to the right of the needle.

2. Place a piece of masking tape on the machine along the right side of the ruler.

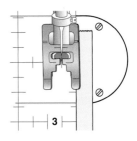

3. Cut two 3" squares and sew them together, using the edge of the tape as your seam guide. Press the seam allowance to one side and press the patches open. Measure the finished piece with your rotary-cutting ruler. It should measure *exactly* 5½" wide. If it doesn't, reposition the marking tape and do the sewing test again. If your patchwork is narrower than 5½", you need to make your seam allowance slightly smaller. If your sample is wider than 5½", your seam is too narrow, so make it a bit wider.

Chain Piecing

Even though as quilters we like cutting our fabric into small pieces and sewing them back together, let's admit it: sometimes sewing the patches of the same two fabrics together to make hundreds of triangle squares or four patches can be pretty tedious. That's where chain piecing comes in. It makes efficient use of your time and saves thread in the process.

In chain piecing, multiple units are passed through the machine without lifting the presser foot and without clipping the threads after each one. The machine continues to sew through a small amount of empty space between each unit. This creates a chain of stitching that is later cut, separating each unit. Often the trickiest part of chain sewing is getting started. Depending on how temperamental your machine is, you may wind up with snarled threads or uneven stitches when you start to sew. There's an easy way to avoid that situation: use a piece of scrap cloth to make the first few inches of stitching.

Start sewing in the middle of the scrap so that the very first stitch is into fabric, not an empty space.

When you reach the end of the scrap, feed the first pair of patches under the presser foot. Continue sewing the patches, and when you reach the last one, cut your scrap of fabric off of the beginning of the chain and feed it through the machine again. Stop with the needle down in the scrap fabric, snip off the actual patchwork pieces, and cut them apart. Leave your scrap in the machine, and you'll be all set for your next round of chain piecing. You can use the same scrap fabric over and over until it is too built up with thread. Simply toss it and start a new one.

Begin sewing with a
scrap starter patch.

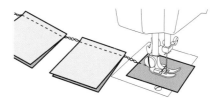

Chain piece units and end
sewing with a fabric scrap.

33

Pinning

Some people like to pin, and others don't. Understanding how a sewing machine works will help you decide whether or not to pin. When sewing two layers of fabric, the bottom layer of fabric is fed into the machine faster than the top layer due to the feed dogs pulling it along. If you sew two long strips that are the same length and you don't pin them, it is almost inevitable that you will end up with leftover fabric on top. Therefore, I think it is important to pin longer seams.

Use fine silk pins, since they allow the fabric to lie flat against the machine. Remove the pin just before you come to it. Some people like to sew over pins, but this causes distortion of both the fabric and the seam. Also, if your sewing-machine needle hits a pin, you can bend or break the needle and adversely affect the timing of the machine.

Matching Straight Seams

Because seams in quiltmaking are generally pressed to one side rather than open, it's a good idea to press in opposite directions seams that will later be joined. This will

reduce bulk and make it much easier for you to sew over the adjoining seam allowances accurately. (For more on pressing, see the chapter "Pressing" on page 45.)

1. Nest or "marry" your seams by having one seam go in one direction and the other seam in the opposite direction. With your fingers, slide the two pieces of patchwork until you feel the seam allowances butt up against one another. They are now in perfect alignment for sewing.

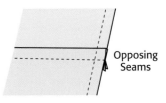
Opposing Seams

2. Pin the seams in place before sewing.
3. Sew with the seam allowances positioned so that the top one will feed through the machine first and the bottom one will follow. This is helpful for two reasons. When the presser foot hits the added bulk of the top seam allowance, it will help push the fabric forward until it is butted tightly against the bottom seam allowance. In addition, with the bottom seam

allowance facing you rather than feeding into the machine first, it won't be likely to get caught up in the feed dogs.

4. Use the tip of your seam ripper instead of your finger to hold the seam allowance in place before it goes under the presser foot. The tip will fit near the presser foot much more easily than your finger will, and you won't risk sewing over your finger.

⬥ AVOIDING ⬥ SHOW-THROUGH

In some instances, butting the seam allowances isn't a good choice. For example, if you press a dark fabric toward a light seam, the dark fabric may be so noticeable that you will not be happy with the results. In this case, you'll have three options for dealing with the situation:

- You can press the seams open.
- You can press both seams toward the dark fabric and have all four seam allowances going in the same direction, even though they'll be bulky.
- You can trim some of the excess darker seam allowance so that it doesn't show up as much.

Matching Points

Patchwork points look beautiful when they are precise and the tip of the point is intact where it joins the adjacent piece. If the seam is sewn too wide, the point will be cut off and look blunt. If the seam is too narrow, the point will not meet the adjacent piece and will look as if it is floating on the background fabric.

When sewing pieces together that will form a point, the intersecting seam lines form an X on the wrong side of the fabric. Try to sew the seam with the X side facing up so that you can see it. To be more precise, spear the X vertically with a pin, and then pin the patches together on either side of the intersection. Carefully sew, removing the pins as you come to them.

This same technique works with matching several intersections. If you have an X on both the top and bottom patches, spear through the top X and check underneath to make sure the pin has hit the mark there as well. If not, adjust the alignment, and then pin the patches together on either side of the crucial intersection.

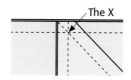

The X

Easing In Excess

Try as we might to cut and sew everything perfectly, there are definitely times when easing pieces to fit is necessary. If you have a significant amount of excess fabric, the seam will look puckered and ruffled, and your option is to rip out the previous sewing and start over. However, a small amount of extra fabric can be eased in successfully. By small, I mean that you can usually ease in about an extra ¼" along the edge of a quilt block. If you're working with borders, then you have a much longer seam and you may find it possible to ease in 1" to 2" along the length of the quilt top.

For best results when easing, have the piece with the extra fullness on the bottom for sewing. The feed dogs will gently ease it in. If the excess fabric is on top, it's much more likely that the presser foot will turn it into pleats. Pin carefully, distributing the fullness evenly along the length of the fabric.

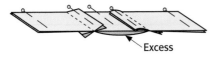

Excess

The feed dogs can also help when sewing a straight-grain edge to a bias edge. Place the bias piece underneath and sew carefully, trying not to pull or stretch the edge. The feed dogs will pull it through the machine evenly, whereas the presser foot will more than likely push it along and stretch the fabric slightly.

Set-In Seams

The construction of some blocks involves the joining of three pieces or units into a Y-shaped formation. This is called a set-in seam and needs to be sewn in two stages. One familiar block that uses set-in seams is an Eight-Pointed Star, also called a LeMoyne Star. As you can see, it's made of parallelograms (diamonds), right triangles, and squares.

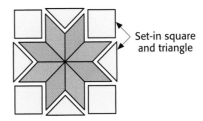

Set-in square and triangle

Sewing pieces with a set-in seam requires that you start and stop stitching the seams ¼" away from the edge of the fabric, leaving the seam allowances free so that the patches can then be sewn to the third patch without forming a pucker or pleat. The key to success is to mark the stopping points precisely and not sew beyond them into the seam allowance area.

1. On the corner of each patch that will be part of the set-in seam area, measure in ¼" from the outer edge and mark a stopping point on the wrong side of the fabric, as shown.

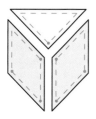

2. Place the first two pieces to be sewn together—a diamond and a triangle—with right sides facing. Use a pin to match the dots, and then pin the remainder of the seam.

3. Start sewing *exactly* on a dot. Take two stitches, and then backstitch two stitches. Sew the remainder of the seam.

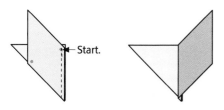

4. Now sew the second diamond to the other short side of the triangle. Start by pinning through the dots, and then pin the remainder of the seam. Begin sewing at a dot, take two stitches, and backstitch as before. Continue sewing the seam.

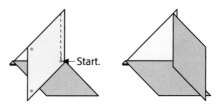

5. Finally, match the points on the diamonds, pin the seam, and stitch as before.

6. Press the unit, pressing the triangle seam allowances toward the diamonds and the two-diamond seam toward one of the diamonds.

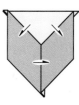

If you have a pucker at the center of the Y-seam formation, it's because you've sewn one of the seams too far. You may need to rip out one or two stitches to alleviate the problem. Press after taking out the stitch and see whether it makes a difference. Sometimes merely pressing the seam allowance between the diamonds in the opposite direction will make the problem disappear.

~ OPEN-TOE ~ PRESSER FOOT

Because you need to see exactly where to start and stop sewing when stitching set-in seams, you might find it handy to use an open-toe presser foot. This attachment will give you a clear view of your starting and stopping points. Just remember, this presser foot probably won't be ¼" wide, so if you are accustomed to using your presser foot as a seam guide, you'll need a backup plan when using an open-toe foot!

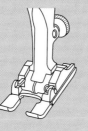

Open-Toe Foot

Partial Seams

Some blocks look trickier to make than they actually are. If you're making a block that has a center shape, such as square, rectangle, or hexagon, with pieces attached to

each side of it that extend beyond the center patch, the block may seem as if a set-in seam or two is required. But take a closer look. You may be able to stitch the block much more easily by using a partial-seam technique. When you attach the first piece to the center patch, sew the seam only halfway. Then you can attach all the other pieces with a full seam. To finish the block, return to the first seam and complete it. It couldn't be easier.

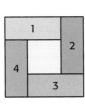
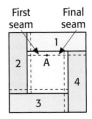

Bright Hopes Block

1. Lay out the block pieces according to the finished block plan.
2. Sew piece 1 partially to the center square, stopping at point A.
3. Sew piece 2 to the unit, followed by piece 3 and piece 4. Press all seams away from the center square.
4. After piece 4 has been added, go back and complete the seam for piece 1.

Here are some other blocks that can also be stitched with partial seams rather than set-in seams.

Arabic Lattice Block

Quarter Star Block

Double Star Block

Curved Seams

Curved seams are really quite manageable, provided you know some tricks for getting them just right. It takes a bit longer to cut the pieces, but the overall effect of the finished piece is well worth the effort. Here are some pointers for sewing curves:

• Fold each piece in half and finger-press a crease perpendicular to the seam line. Make sure to match these creases when pinning and sewing.

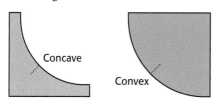
Concave

Convex

Crease centers.

• Some people like to have the convex piece on the bottom, and others like to have the concave piece on the bottom. When the convex piece is on the bottom, you can use the stretch in the concave curve to ease it gently around the convex piece. Conversely, with the concave piece on the bottom, the feed dogs help to ease in what seems like extra fabric. Experiment to see which method you prefer.

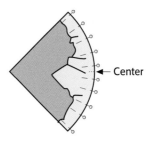
← Center

• Set the stitch length on the machine a little longer than normal; you may find it helps when easing the pieces together.

• Always stop sewing with the needle in the down position. This will help keep the pieces from slipping while you manipulate them with your hands.

• Sew slowly to give more time for your hands to control the fabric.

• To make sure you sew an accurate ¼" seam over the entire curve, try to keep the fabric edges together at all times. For some quilters, pinning at regular intervals helps. Others find it easier to pin just at the ends and in the center, and then they use their fingers or a stiletto to manipulate the fabric as they stitch the curve.

- Press the finished seams toward the concave curve. For gentle curves, you shouldn't have to clip the seams to make them lie flat.

Foundation Piecing

Some quiltmakers love foundation piecing because it affords a way to make intricately pieced blocks that would otherwise require lots of template making and hand piecing to get the pieces to align precisely. With foundation piecing, the patches are sewn to a paper or fabric foundation that is marked with the block pattern. The foundation stabilizes the patchwork, making it easier to sew long narrow points or other irregular-shaped pieces together accurately. Once you get the knack for foundation piecing, it can be quite fun. However, it can be a little confusing at first. So here are some tips to help you avoid the frustrations that can cause setbacks to the novice foundation piecer:

- Usually used for blocks with many small pieces, the pieces of fabric are placed wrong side down on a foundation fabric, stitched, turned right side up, and pressed. You can make your own patterns on paper or muslin, or you can buy them with the patterns already printed on paper or muslin.

- Choose the right foundation for your project. You can use muslin, which will remain in your quilt and add a layer of bulk. This is a time-honored technique. However, if you don't want the extra fabric in your quilt, use paper foundations; after all the stitching is complete, the papers are torn away.

- Make sure the foundations are accurate. If you use a photocopier to make multiple copies, measure the finished patterns to confirm that they haven't been distorted in the copying process.

- If you make your own copies, it's a good idea to write the sewing order on the foundations. Purchased foundation patterns generally come with the order indicated to help you correctly piece the block.

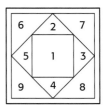

Foundation Pattern

- Set your stitch length to slightly shorter than normal. When you remove the foundation papers, you'll run less risk of pulling the stitches out along with the paper.
- Begin with the center piece, or whatever piece is marked with the number 1. Secure this piece to the *wrong* side of the foundation with a pin, making sure that the *wrong* side of the fabric is facing the wrong side of the foundation. Then, working in order, pin the next patch in place, *right side facing the first patch*. From this point on, all new patches will be added right sides together.

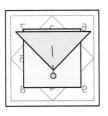

Pieces 1 and 2

- Sew the seams from the printed side of the foundation, sewing exactly on the marked lines. To secure your pieces, start and stop sewing a few stitches beyond the marked line. There is no need to backstitch. Continue adding patches in sequence.

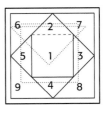

Stitch on
foundation side.

- After adding each patch, go back and trim the seam allowance to ¼". You can simply eyeball the measurement and trim the excess with scissors, or you can fold the foundation and excess fabric out of the way and use your rotary cutter and ruler to trim an exact ¼".

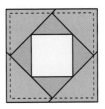

Finished Block

⤳ WORK THE ANGLES ⤳

One of the trickiest things about foundation piecing is sewing a patch to cover an odd-shaped area, and then opening the sewn piece only to discover it doesn't quite cover the intended area. Here are my tips for preventing this from happening in the first place and for an easy way to fix it if it does happen.

Adequate coverage. If you need a patch to cover an angled shape on the foundation, it's easy to get the angle backwards and, as a result, to have a patch that folds out in the opposite direction of the way you want it to go. To avoid this problem, make sure you cut a large enough piece of fabric to cover the intended area. Before sewing, lay the patch *right side up* over the *wrong* side of the foundation to make sure it completely covers the area and allows enough excess for the seam allowances. Now flip the piece over along the edge that will be the first to be stitched. Then simply slide it over so that you have approximately ¼" of it covering the seam allowance area. Pin it in place, even though it may look like it doesn't fit. Turn the foundation paper over, stitch along the seam line, and fold open the patch. Voilà—you should have a perfect fit.

Fixing mistakes. If you should happen to sew the patch at the wrong spot or sew it so that it doesn't completely cover its intended area, it can be nearly impossible to tear out the stitching without ruining the paper foundation (especially if you're using a shorter stitch length). Instead of using the seam ripper, use your fabric scissors to trim away the seam allowance of the offending fabric only. Cut as close as possible to your line of stitching. Now tug on the remaining part of the fabric. It should pull away from the stitching line, leaving only the sewing line and a few stray threads. Cut a new piece of fabric to fit the space; resew, stitching just inside the first line of stitching, to correct your mistake.

English Paper Piecing

English paper piecing is a hand-sewing technique that is a good alternative to machine sewing set-in seams. With this method, the quilt patches are basted onto paper foundations. The papers remain attached until the pieces are sewn together, giving stability and precision to your work. This technique requires up-front preparation, but once that's done, the project will be completely portable—no sewing machine required.

Shapes such as hexagons for Grandmother's Flower Garden quilts or diamonds for Eight-Pointed Stars are good candidates for English paper piecing. You can purchase precut paper foundations in a variety of shapes and sizes, or you can make your own.

Lightweight card stock makes good foundations, as does freezer paper. With freezer paper, you can iron the foundations onto your fabrics and cut around them, rather than marking around them with a pencil. The following steps describe the process of English paper piecing:

1. If you're making your own paper foundations, make a master template out of template plastic. The template should be the finished size (without seam allowances added). Then trace around this plastic template onto your card stock or freezer paper. Cut out the paper foundations (one for each piece in your quilt or block), trimming each one just to the inside of your drawn line. If you cut outside the lines, by the time you account for the fabric being folded over the foundation, your patches will grow in size.

2. If you're using freezer-paper foundations, place them shiny side down on the wrong side of your fabric. The pieces need to be spaced far enough apart so that you can cut a ¼" seam allowance around each foundation. Press with a dry iron to adhere the foundations to the fabric. Rotary cut fabric pieces ¼" beyond each edge of the paper.

   If you're using card stock, trace around the shapes onto the wrong side of the fabric, again leaving at least ½" between them so that each can accommodate ¼" seam allowances. Cut out the shapes, trimming roughly ¼" from the drawn lines.

3. With the paper side facing you, fold the seam allowance over the paper and baste the seam allowance in place, stitching through the paper.

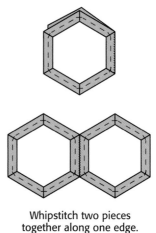

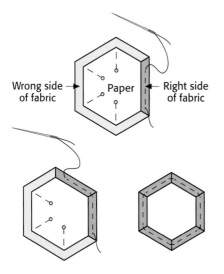

Wrong side of fabric → Paper ←Right side of fabric

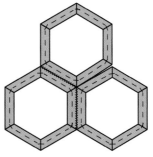

Whipstitch two pieces together along one edge.

4. To sew the pieces together, hold two of them right sides together with the edges even. Using a double strand of thread, whip-stitch the pieces together along the fold, using small stitches and taking care to not stitch through the paper. You can take an extra stitch or two at the end of the seam to secure it, and then con-tinue sewing, adding the next piece.

Stitch the next piece to the first two.

5. When all pieces are joined, remove the basting stitches and papers and press the patchwork. If you're working on a large quilt, the papers can make it quite heavy to hold in your lap. If desired, you can remove the papers once all sides of a partic-ular piece have been stitched in place, rather than waiting until the entire quilt top has been pieced.

CHAPTER 5

PRESSING

NEVER UNDERESTIMATE THE VALUE OF GOOD
PRESSING IN YOUR QUILTMAKING. IF YOU CUT AND
SEW ACCURATELY BUT DON'T TAKE THE TIME TO
PRESS CORRECTLY, YOUR PATCHWORK CAN END UP
JUST AS OFF-KILTER AS IT WOULD IF YOU HAD
GONE AWRY IN THE CUTTING OR STITCHING. IN
SHORT, THE WAY YOU PRESS CAN MAKE OR BREAK
YOUR FINISHED QUILT TOP.

First of all, pressing is not ironing. Pressing entails gently lowering and lifting the iron. Ironing is a more aggressive back-and-forth motion of the iron along the fabric that can pull and distort shapes. Pressing, on the other hand, lets you turn seam allowances to one side without distorting your patchwork or appliqué shapes.

For years, quilters have bandied about certain rules of pressing. It often makes sense to apply these rules, such as "press toward the darker fabric." But there are times when a particular rule is just not the best option for the project you're sewing. Instead, here are some guidelines to help you press for success—in any situation.

- Press each seam before you sew that unit to another piece. This will help you avoid mismatched seams or stitched-in pleats.
- Always set the seam by pressing the piece with right sides together, just as you sewed them. Your finished patchwork will appear much smoother and neater if you do.

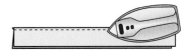

Press, lift, move, and lower
the iron along the seam.

- After setting the seam, open the piece on top and press gently along the seam line. This will ensure that your seam allowance is pressed to one side. Press toward

45

the darker color—if it makes sense. To do so, start with the darker fabric on top, open up the dark patch or strip, and press.

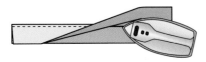

Flip top fabric over and press.

- Sometimes pressing toward the dark fabric isn't feasible because you'll be creating too much bulk once the seam is joined with another one that has the seam allowance pressed in the same direction. If you need to press toward the light fabric, check the finished work from the right side. If you can see the darker fabric showing through the lighter one, trim the darker seam allowance to slightly less than ¼" to make it less noticeable.
- Some seams tend to gravitate toward a certain side. Listen to what they are saying.
- Pressing a seam toward one side or the other can often make a big difference in the appearance of your patchwork. When sewing triangle squares together, for instance, open up the pieces and take a look at them from the right side. Notice that if you fold the seam allowance to one side, it looks as if you haven't quite met the mark where the points are to join. Fold the seam allowance in the opposite direction, and the points may match perfectly. Once you determine the best direction, press the seam accordingly.
- Some quilters love using steam; others would never dream of using it. If your iron has a steam button, you can use a shot of intentionally placed steam to coax a stubborn seam into submission, but let the pieces cool on the ironing board. If you pick them up and move them while damp, you might stretch them out of shape.
- If you press a seam and then decide that you want it to go in the opposite direction, "unpress" it by pressing it in the closed position to reset the seam. Then press it in the desired direction.

∼ MAGIC SIZING ∼
TO THE RESCUE

I love to use Magic Sizing when I press. It adds a certain element of crispness to the pieces, and I think it helps make things nice and square. (I also like the smell!) Just take care when using spray sizing. It dampens your fabric, so press carefully; you don't want to stretch the pieces out of shape.

Finger-Pressing

In a pinch, you can substitute finger-pressing for pressing with an iron. If you don't feel like constantly hopping up to get to the iron while creating a block, place the piece on a hard surface, right side up. Using the underside of your thumbnail, firmly draw it along the seam but hold the fabric steady with your other hand so that you don't stretch the fabric. If you do a lot of finger-pressing, you can purchase a handy little tool for this purpose at most quilt shops.

Planning for Pressing

Having a pressing plan before you begin sewing will be helpful in making sure your seams butt neatly at intersections, thus allowing the finished quilt top to lie flat and smooth. The bottom line is to have the bulk of seams spread out; one should lie to the right and the other to the left. Let's take a look at a Nine Patch block as an example.

One option is to press all the seams in the first row to the left, all the seams in the second row to the right, and all the seams in the third row to the left. Notice that this does not follow the rule of pressing toward the dark, which we said isn't always possible. However, in this situation, the second option would be to press all seams to the darker fabric, and it is possible. In fact, this would be my choice for a Nine Patch block.

Press alternate rows in opposite directions.

Press toward dark fabric.

Admittedly, this is an easy example. Some quilts that have a variety of blocks are not always so easy to figure out. Make a sketch of your finished quilt and try planning your pressing scheme in advance. Pick the most logical approach, remembering that sometimes you might have to press seam allowances toward the light fabric.

47

CHAPTER 6

HAND APPLIQUÉ

THE HUMBLE PRACTICE OF PATCHING WORN SPOTS IN CLOTHING MIGHT BE ONE EXPLANATION FOR THE ORIGIN OF APPLIQUÉ. THE SAME TECHNIQUE— SEWING A SMALL PIECE OF FABRIC TO A BACK- GROUND CLOTH—WAS ELEVATED TO AN ART FORM IN THE MID-NINETEENTH CENTURY BY METHODIST WOMEN IN MARYLAND WHO CREATED THE BEAUTI- FUL AND ELABORATE BALTIMORE ALBUM QUILTS. APPLIQUÉ ALLOWS THE QUILTER TO MAKE INTRICATE DESIGNS WITH CURVES AND SHARP POINTS.

Traditional appliqué is done by hand, but it can also be done by machine or by using fusible web. For more on machine and fusible-web appliqué, see chapter 7 starting on page 64.

Supplies for Hand Appliqué

I love to appliqué, since all I really need in front of me are scissors, thread, a needle, a few pins, and my fabric pieces. My favorite method is to use freezer paper for templates. Once I iron the shapes onto the fabric, I can sit for hours and do the handwork that I love. Or I can put it all in a little plastic bag and take it anywhere.

Fabrics

Traditionally, appliqué background fabrics were usually a light solid color or sometimes a small, light-colored print. Today just about anything goes. A dark fabric with brightly colored appliqués can be quite dramatic, while some prints, plaids, or striped fabrics can be appropriate for a folk-art quilt. Select the background fabric (or use more than one!) based on the statement you want to make with your quilt.

Fabric for the appliqué design must be appropriate for the particular design. Solids and small-scale prints are always safe. Take caution when using large-scale prints. The design will often be lost when the fabric is cut into small pieces. Depending on your quilt, that can be effective if you cut and use a specific portion of the print. In fact, a style of appliqué called *broderie perse* uses this technique exclusively.

In broderie perse, *printed motifs are cut from one fabric and appliquéd onto another.*

Look for prints that have texture to them to give life and dimension to your work. For example, if you are making a leaf, choose a fabric that has several shades of green in it. And depending on the style of your quilt, you can either work in a realistic palette or one that's more whimsical.

The key thing to consider when selecting fabrics for appliqué is how they will handle. If they are too loosely woven, they may be limp and fray. If they are too stiff, it will be difficult to turn under the seam allowance. You can give body to limp fabrics with a bit of spray sizing; however, you'll need to wash your finished quilt to remove the sizing. Also note that synthetic fabrics are hard to work with because their edges tend to fray more readily than those of 100%-cotton fabrics.

Needles

The needles you use for hand appliqué should be thin enough to glide through the fabric effortlessly so that you can make tiny, invisible stitches. Size 10 or 12 is a good choice, with the larger number being the finer needle.

The length of the needle is an individual preference. The shortest needle is called a Between and is generally used for hand quilting. The next-longest size is called a Sharp; these are popular for appliqué. A crewel needle is longer still, and the longest is called a milliner's or straw needle. Some quilters prefer longer needles for turning under the edges of the appliqué pieces, while others find shorter needles easier to manipulate. I personally prefer a straw needle for both basting and appliquéing.

Thread

Thread color should match the appliqué piece, not the background fabric. Two popular choices are 100%-cotton thread and 100%-silk thread. Silk thread is finer and nearly invisible after stitching. However, each type of thread has its advocates. Cotton thread may be easier to find and match to your fabric colors, and some quilters like all the fibers in their quilts to be the same—100% cotton.

If you baste your pieces in place, use light-colored thread so that you don't run the risk of a stray bit of dark thread being left between your quilt layers where it can show through or even bleed onto your lighter fabric.

Pins

Use small, straight pins, ½" to ¾" long, because they're less likely to get in your way or tangle your thread as you sew.

Scissors

Sharp-bladed scissors that cut right to the point are a must for fine hand appliqué. You'll need them for trimming threads, seam allowances, inner points, and curves.

Glue Stick

Some quilters like to use a fabric glue stick to hold appliqué pieces in place instead of basting. If you use glue, you'll need to wash the finished quilt to remove it, so be sure your fabrics are prewashed so that they won't shrink or bleed in your finished quilt.

Template Plastic and Permanent Marker

Clear or translucent template plastic is perfect for making appliqué templates. You can trace designs from books or patterns or make your own original designs. Template plastic is quite durable, so you can trace around the same template many times while maintaining accuracy. Once the templates are marked and cut, you can trace around them directly onto your fabric for needle-turn appliqué or onto freezer paper if you prefer that method of appliqué.

Use a fine-point permanent marker or a fabric pencil to trace around templates for needle-turn appliqué.

50

In a pinch, you can make templates out of cardboard. Cardboard isn't as durable as template plastic, so it's best to use it if you only need a few appliqués of a particular shape. With repeated tracings, the edges will wear away and make your shapes a little less accurate.

Freezer Paper

Even if you never intend on wrapping meat for the freezer, this plastic-coated paper on a roll is a must have. It's available in grocery stores—look for it in the plastic-wrap aisle. You can draw and write on the plain white side of the paper, and then iron it, coated side down, onto your appliqué fabric. It will stick in place so that you can use it as a cutting template or as a guide for turning under edges.

Silver Marking Pencil

Some quilters like to mark the appliqué placement on the background fabric, while others simply fold the background square to mark the center point. If you prefer marked guidelines, I highly recommend using a silver marking pencil. It is dark enough to be visible but will wash out.

Preparing the Background

There are two schools of thought when it comes to preparing the background for appliqué. Some quilters like to mark the complete design on the background fabric as a placement guide, while others prefer just a few simple markings, such as the center of the block or outer edges of the block. In the following section, we'll review how to mark the design onto your fabric if that's your preference. Then we'll discuss how to make a clear overlay to use as a placement guide so that you don't have to mark your fabric.

With either method, the first step is to cut your background squares, rectangles, or whatever shapes you need. Cut these pieces oversize (½" to 1" larger in each direction), as sometimes appliquéing onto them can draw up the fabric and make them shrink a bit. When all the appliqué work is complete, you can trim the block to size.

Marking the Background Fabric

Find the center of your background fabric and appliqué pattern by folding them in quarters. Mark the center intersection and line them up when positioning the fabric over the pattern.

If your background fabric is light colored, position it over the pattern or design, right side up, and trace the design with a silver marking pencil. To prevent shifting, tape both the pattern and the fabric in position. For dark-colored background fabric, use a light box, or tape the design to a sunlit window and trace the design.

If you are worried that your markings for the design will still be visible after you attach the appliqué pieces, trace slightly *inside* the design lines. This way your pieces will cover the markings and you won't have to worry about them showing or about how to remove the markings.

Using an Overlay

As an alternative to marking the background fabric, you can use a clear plastic or acetate overlay as a placement guide. Acetate sheets are available at office-supply stores. Place a sheet of acetate over the appliqué pattern or design and trace it onto the acetate with a permanent marker. Mark the center point of the design on the acetate, too.

Tape the edges of the background fabric on your work table. Then place the overlay on top of your background fabric, aligning the center points. Tape the overlay in place along the top edge of the fabric only. Once your appliqué shapes are prepared, you can lift the overlay, slip the appliqués in place, and then flip the overlay back in place to check for placement. Move the pieces as necessary and then pin in place.

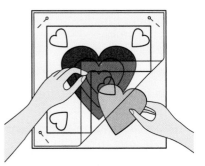

Slide appliqué shapes under the overlay to place them on the background.

Making Templates for the Appliqués

Mark each shape on template plastic. Do not add a seam allowance. Cut out each shape exactly on the marked line; it is the finished size. Write the name of the pattern or shape on the right side of the template. This will not only indicate which side of the template to use, but it will also help you keep track of your pattern pieces.

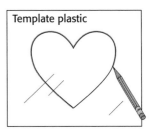

Template plastic

Once you make your templates, how you mark and cut your fabric depends on the method of appliqué you plan to do. In the following sections, we'll review needle-turn appliqué and freezer-paper appliqué—using the freezer paper as a template on top of fabric as well as underneath. Each method has its followers and yields nice results, so choose the method that works best for you.

Needle-Turn Appliqué

With this method, you mark the shape directly onto the right side of the fabric and turn under the edges as you go, using the tip of the needle to help you turn the edges.

Cutting Appliqué Pieces

1. Place the template right side up on the right side of the fabric.
2. Mark around the template with a fine-lead mechanical pencil, a piece of sharpened chalk, or even a fine-point permanent marker such as a Pigma pen. When marking several shapes at once on one piece of fabric, make sure to leave at least ½" between each shape for seam allowances.
3. Cut out each piece, adding a ¼" seam allowance all around the edges.

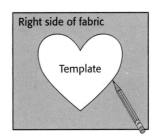
Right side of fabric
Template

〜 GOING WITH THE GRAIN 〜

Grain line is not quite as important with appliqué as it is with patchwork. A traditional rule has been to cut pieces so that when they are sewn to background fabric, the grain line of the appliqué is the same as the grain line of the background. However, if you want to take advantage of a particular part of a print or plaid, you can go against the grain and cut as desired. Here are some other tips about working with grain line in appliqué.

- When using a large print, you may want to cut from a specific part so that a design will be centered. In this case, you may disregard grain line.
- Try to cut curved shapes with as much of the curve on the bias as is possible. This reduces the chances of the edges fraying and also makes turning under the curves easier.
- Pieces with sharp points should be cut so that the points are on the bias as shown.

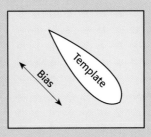

- Shapes that have straight edges, such as a flat-bottomed basket, are easier to appliqué if the straight edge is cut along the straight grain of the fabric. Of course, if you're using a plaid or stripe and prefer that it be cut on the bias so that the stripes in the fabric resemble a basket weave, cut the fabric accordingly. Just take care not to stretch the fabric out of shape as you sew the bias edge.

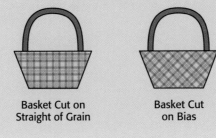

Basket Cut on
Straight of Grain

Basket Cut
on Bias

Appliquéing the Block

1. Pin or baste the appliqué pieces to the background fabric in the correct position, taking care that they don't extend into the block's ¼" seam allowance. If you have layered pieces in your block, start with the bottom pieces. The other pieces can be added after the bottom layers are stitched in place.

2. Use the tip of your needle to turn under the seam allowance. Hold the turned-under edge in place with your thumb and fore-finger as you stitch the piece to the background. Turn under about ½" of the seam allowance at a time. Working with just a small portion of the seam at a time helps you form a smooth edge, even along the curves. Refer to "The Traditional Appliqué Stitch" on page 56 for details on making small, evenly spaced stitches.

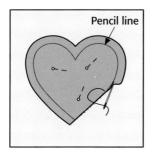

Pencil line

3. For any area that will be covered by another appliqué shape, you do not need to turn under the seam allowance. You can just baste that portion in place since it will be covered later. This will help reduce bulk in your fin-ished piece.

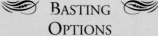 BASTING OPTIONS

When project directions say to baste the appliqué pieces in place, you have several options.

- Pin pieces securely, making sure the pins will not interfere with your stitching. Sometimes pinning from the wrong side will help prevent your thread from snagging on the pins as you sew.

- Hand baste the pieces. This takes a little more time, but there will be no pins getting in your way.

- Use a water-soluble glue stick to hold the pieces in place. Apply the glue only to the middle of the piece and not around the outside edges where you will be sewing. If you use glue, you'll need to rinse it out when your quilt is complete, so be sure you've prewashed your fabrics.

The Traditional Appliqué Stitch

This method works well on all shapes, whether you baste the edges in place or turn them under as you go. A heart is a good shape for practicing appliqué, no matter what method of appliqué you choose. A heart has straight edges, curves, outside points, and inside points, so with one familiar shape you can learn all the aspects of appliqué!

1. Use a single strand of thread about 18" long. Thread the needle and make a knot at one end. Insert the needle into the back side of the appliqué piece through the seam allowance so that it comes out to the right side at the fold line. It's best to start stitching along a straight edge or a gentle curve rather than at a sharp curve or point.

2. Begin by inserting your needle into the background fabric, and then let it travel under the wrong side of the background fabric parallel to the appliqué piece. Bring it up about ⅛" away from the first stitch, catching just a few threads of the appliqué piece along the fold.

Right handers, stitch from right to left; left handers, stitch from left to right.

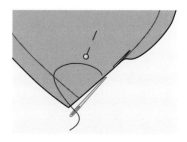

3. Make the next stitch by inserting the needle into the background fabric right next to the place where it came through the appliqué piece. Do not slant the stitch down; make it exactly horizontal to your fabrics. The tip of the needle should travel under the fabric another ⅛"; bring it up through a few threads of the appliqué piece along the fold.

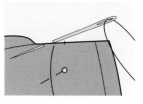

Appliqué Stitch

4. Gently tug each stitch to make sure it is snug but not so tight as to cause distortion.

5. Keep stitching in the above manner, making the length of the stitches consistent. It is sometimes necessary to shorten the stitches a little to accommodate curves. For more on curves, see "Clipping Curves for Appliqué" on page 58.

6. When you reach an inside point, clip the fabric to the point so that you can splay the seam allowance in the two opposite directions.

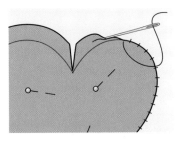

7. For the outer points, fold under the seam allowance on one side of the point and stitch in place all the way to the point. Take an extra stitch right at the point, then trim away excess fabric in the seam allowance and fold under the seam allowance on the second side of the point. Continue stitching as before.

8. To end, pull the needle and thread through to the wrong side of the background fabric and make two small knots by pulling your thread through a loop. After you make the knot, run the thread between the background fabric and appliqué piece for about 2". Bring the needle up and clip the thread close to the appliqué.

Back of appliqué block

≈ HINTS FOR ≈ SMOOTH STITCHING

- Use your needle to push down any little points of fabric that are making bumps along the curved edge of the appliqué piece.
- Use smaller stitches near points to keep any frayed edges from escaping.
- Make a straight stitch directly at an inside point to help emphasize its shape.

≈ CLIPPING ≈ CURVES FOR APPLIQUÉ

Sometimes it is necessary to clip the inside or concave curves in an appliqué piece to make the piece lie flat and smooth. If you clip too deeply, it will weaken your fabric and make it hard to turn under an edge that won't have a raw edge showing. Clip only halfway to the seam line.

If you find that you're still having difficulty turning the edge under smoothly, trim away part of the seam allowance so that you have closer to a ⅛" allowance instead of ¼". Note that you should not clip outside or convex curves, since that will result in a bumpy-looking curve.

Freezer-Paper Appliqué

Many quiltmakers like to use freezer paper to prepare their appliqué shapes. It gives the pieces stability and a crisp edge for turning under seam allowances. You can work with freezer paper two ways.

First, you can press the freezer paper to the right side of the appliqué fabric and use the edge of the paper as a turn-under guide for needle-turn appliqué. Or, you can press it to the wrong side of the fabric shape and then turn the seam allowances back over the edge of the paper and hand baste them in place.

Freezer Paper on Top

If you plan to appliqué with the freezer-paper shapes on top, simply use your plastic appliqué templates to trace the designs onto the uncoated side of the freezer paper. Cut out the shapes exactly on the line. Press these shapes onto the

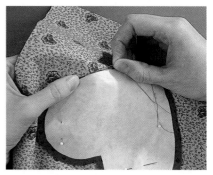

Turn under the fabric seam allowance along the crisp edge of the freezer paper as you go.

right side of your selected fabric, cut the fabric out approximately ¼" from the edge of the paper shape, and position your shapes on the background. Appliqué as described in "Needle-Turn Appliqué" on page 53 and peel the freezer paper off when each shape is complete.

Freezer-paper shapes can be used several times before they will no longer stick to your fabric.

Freezer Paper on the Bottom

For freezer paper on the bottom, follow these steps to prepare your shapes.

1. Trace a mirror image of each shape onto the uncoated side of the freezer paper. For symmetrical shapes, this isn't a concern, but if your shape is asymmetrical, flip the plastic template right side down onto the freezer paper before tracing. You need the image to be reversed because you'll be pressing it to the wrong side of your fabric, where it will be upside down as you appliqué.

2. Cut out each shape exactly on the drawn line; do not add seam allowances.

3. Place the coated side of the freezer paper on the wrong side of the appliqué fabric and press with a dry iron. The freezer paper will adhere to the fabric.

4. Cut out the shape, adding a ¼" seam allowance around the paper as you cut.

With this method, the entire seam allowance is turned under first and basted in place.

5. Turn the seam allowance under, toward the freezer paper, and baste it in place by hand. The basting will go through the paper. Make sure the seam allowance is turned right at the edge of the paper. Too loose and you won't have a smooth edge. Too tight and your paper will curl and not lie flat.

Fold.

When you get to a curve, do not baste through the freezer paper. Instead, take small running stitches in the seam allowance of the fabric only. Once you have stitched past the curve, gently tug the thread to pull up the stitches a bit, and the fabric will magically conform to the curve of the freezer paper. Continue basting the rest of the shape by going through the fabric and freezer paper.

6. Sew the appliqués to the background with the traditional appliqué stitch described on page 56. When the appliqué work is complete, remove the basting. Then make a small slit in the background fabric behind the appliqué shape so that you can remove the freezer paper. A seam ripper works well to make the initial small cut. Then use scissors to make the slit longer.

If you prefer not to slit the background fabric, you can either use the freezer-paper-on-the-top method or stitch almost all the way around a shape, leaving about ½" unsewn. Remove the basting and use tweezers to reach under the appliqué shape to grab the freezer paper and pull it out. Fold the seam allowance back in place and resume stitching.

Making Circles for Appliqué

Many appliqué patterns call for circles, from flower centers to bunches of grapes. There's no need to avoid these beautiful patterns because of the circles. Here's how to make them neatly and precisely.

You'll need a template to help you turn under the circle edges, and freezer paper generally isn't heavy enough for this job. I use the cardboard from cereal boxes or manila folders. The more precise your template, the more perfect your finished appliqué circles will look. I like to use a handy circle-maker plastic template from Rapidesign. I purchased mine in the art department of a local bookstore, but you can find them at art-supply and office-supply stores too. It is a plastic template with circle cutouts ranging in size from 2 to 50 millimeters (roughly ⅛" to 2" in diameter).

1. Find the circle on the template that is the exact size of the circle from your appliqué design. Run a pencil around the circle to draw it on your cardboard, and then cut out the circle. You can make several circle cardboard templates or use the same circle over and over.

2. Now find the circle on the template that is the size of your appliqué design plus a generous ¼" seam allowance. Trace these circles on your appliqué fabric and cut out the circles on each line.

3. Thread a needle but do not tie a knot. Baste a running stitch around the circle of fabric, leaving a tail about 3" long at the beginning and another tail about 3" long at the end.

4. With the wrong side of the fabric facing up, place the cardboard circle in the middle of the fabric circle. Pull both sides of the basting thread until the fabric gathers and molds around the cardboard circle.

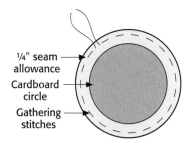

¼" seam allowance

Cardboard circle

Gathering stitches

5. Turn the piece over and press with a steam iron. Let the piece dry and cool, and then gently pull a bit of the stitching open until you can reach in and remove the cardboard circle. Repress the seam allowance, being careful not to burn your fingers. Remove the basting threads, and then appliqué the circles in place.

Making Stems and Vines for Appliqué

Many traditional appliqué designs use stems or vines, which are generally anywhere from ⅛" to ½" in width. In order to make these narrow fabric strips bend and meander, the fabric must be cut on the bias—a 45° angle to the selvage of your fabric. I have a favorite green print that I use quite often for stems, so I cut many long lengths at one time and have them on hand for whenever I need an appliqué vine.

Folded Stem Method

This is my favorite method and one that I learned in a quilting class with noted quiltmaker and author, Mimi Dietrich.

1. Cut a bias strip four times the finished width of the stem or vine. If your finished stem needs to be ¼" wide, then cut a bias strip 1" wide.

2. Fold the strip in half lengthwise, wrong sides together. Press.

Fold strip in half lengthwise.

3. From the strip, cut a stem the length required plus about ½" extra for tucking under at the ends.

4. Place the stem so that the raw edges are aligned with the marked stem or vine line on your background fabric. If the strip is very long, you may want to use pins to hold it in place. I have found that if a strip is short, my fingers can easily keep it where I want it. Because the strip is cut on the bias, it will ease smoothly around any curves.

5. Thread the needle with a color that matches the strip and knot one end. Starting at one end of the strip, use small running stitches to sew it to the background fabric. Stitch along the middle of the strip, sewing a scant bit closer to the raw edge than the folded edge. Fasten the end by making a knot, but do not cut your thread.

6. Roll the folded edge of the strip over the stitching to cover the raw edges. Using the thread that is still attached, appliqué the folded edge of the stem to the background. If any raw edges are showing, carefully trim a bit of the seam allowance. Do not turn under or stitch the ends of the stem if other appliqué shapes such as flowers or leaves will cover them.

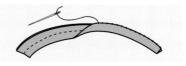

Bias Bar Method

Bias bars are handy tools that let you easily make stems and vines. They come in sets of varying widths and are available in metal or nylon.

1. Choose the bias bar that corresponds to the finished width of your stems. Then cut your stem fabric on the bias, cutting strips twice as wide as the bias bar, plus ½" for seam allowances.

2. Fold the fabric strip in half lengthwise, *wrong* sides together. Sew a scant ¼" from the raw edges. (If you sew a seam that is too big, your bias bar won't fit in the tube!)

≈ PERFECT FIT ≈ EVERY TIME

Here's an easy way to sew the seam on your bias tube so that you know the bar will fit in it nicely.

1. Replace the presser foot on your machine with the zipper foot. Set the needle position to stitch on the left side of the zipper foot.

2. Lay the bias bar on top of your folded bias strip with the length of the bar aligned with the folded edge of the fabric, and stitch right along the edge of the bar. Be sure to keep the bar even with the fold as you feed the fabric through the machine.

Because you're stitching just to the outside of the bar, the finished tube will be wide enough for the bias bar to slip into.

3. Slide the bias bar inside the fabric tube. Twist the fabric until the seam is centered along one flat side of the bias bar. Press the tube flat, with the seam allowance pressed to one side. If your stem is longer than the bias bar, start pressing at one edge and gently work the bias bar along inside the tube, pressing as you go. Remove the bias bar when the entire tube has been pressed, and then press the tube again. For very narrow stems, you may need to trim the seam allowance so that it won't show on the finished bias stem.

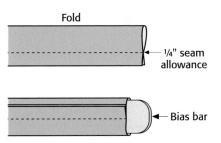

Fold

¼" seam allowance

Bias bar

4. Cut the fabric tube to your required stem lengths, position the cut sections on your background fabric, and appliqué in place along each long edge. Do not turn under the ends if they will be overlapped with other appliqué pieces.

CHAPTER 7

MACHINE APPLIQUÉ

WHILE APPLIQUÉ WAS TRADITIONALLY DONE BY HAND, THERE ARE OTHER OPTIONS FOR TODAY'S QUILTERS THAT TAKE LESS TIME. USING YOUR SEWING MACHINE TO SEW APPLIQUÉ PIECES IN PLACE IS SENSIBLE FOR QUILTS THAT WILL GET QUITE A BIT OF USE AND REQUIRE FREQUENT WASHING. HOW YOU PREPARE THE APPLIQUÉ SHAPES AND WHAT TYPE OF STITCH YOU USE AROUND THEM WILL AFFECT THE LOOK OF YOUR FINISHED PIECE. A FEW DIFFERENT APPROACHES TO THE TECHNIQUE ARE PRESENTED IN THIS CHAPTER.

Fusible Method

The fastest way to prepare appliqué shapes is to trace the shapes onto fusible web, press the webbing onto the wrong side of appliqué fabrics, and cut them out. You can fuse the shapes to the background fabric and then stitch around them to make the appliqués durable for machine washing. Or, skip the stitching for a quick and easy project.

If you want to sew around the edges of the finished appliqués, you'll need lightweight, paper-backed fusible web. If you don't intend to stitch around each shape, choose heavy-duty paper-backed fusible web for extra hold. This type of fusible web has more glue and it will gum up your machine needle if you try to sew through it.

1. Make plastic templates for each shape (see page 52); then trace around the shapes as many times as needed onto the paper-backing side of the fusible web. If your design doesn't use repeated shapes, you can simply trace

each shape directly from the pattern onto the fusible web, eliminating the need to make plastic templates. For patterns that are not symmetrical, make sure you flip the template over and then trace so you have a reversed image.

2. Cut out each shape roughly ¼" outside the lines. Or, if you are cutting several shapes from the same fabric, trace them side by side onto the fusible web, and cut the group out as a unit.

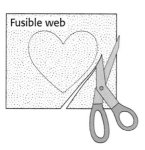

3. Place the fusible-web shapes on the wrong side of your appliqué fabrics. Press, following the manufacturer's instructions.

4. Cut out the appliqué shapes on the traced lines.

5. Remove the paper backing from the shapes and position the appliqués with the web side down on the background fabric. Once you're satisfied with how the appliqués look, press them in place.

6. Machine stitch around the shapes if desired, or just leave them as is. For guidelines on machine stitching, see "Stitching Appliqué by Machine" on page 67.

⚈ Reducing ⚈ Stiffness

Fusible web will cause your appliqués to be a little stiffer than if you hadn't used it. For small shapes, this generally isn't a problem. However, if you are fusing large appliqué shapes or multiple-layered shapes, fusible web can make a quilt top that is less than cuddly.

To reduce the stiffness, trim out the center portion of the fusible-web shape before adhering it to your fabric. After cutting out the shape, use your scissors to trim ¼" inside the drawn lines. This will leave you with about a ½"-wide ring of fusible web to press onto your fabric. It will be enough to let you adhere the shape to the background and stabilize the edges as you stitch them in place.

Freezer-Paper Method

With this method, freezer paper is used to stabilize the appliqué shapes so that you can sew through them without stretching them out of shape.

1. Trace the appliqué shapes onto the uncoated side of the freezer paper. Cut out each shape exactly on the line.

2. Place the freezer-paper shapes on the wrong side of your appliqué fabrics, shiny side up. Pin them in place, and then cut out the fabric shapes, adding a ¼" seam allowance around all the edges.

Cut ¼" from outside edge of template.

3. Using the tip of a dry iron, turn the seam allowances over the paper patterns to adhere them to the freezer paper. For points, press the seam allowance in place on one side of the point. Then fold the other side of the point over the freezer paper. Finally, make a fold at the point or corner, trimming excess fabric as needed.

You may need to clip concave curves to get a smooth curve. For convex curves, gently ease in the excess fabric with the tip of your iron. If necessary, trim the seam allowance to about ⅛" so that you have less fabric to ease.

Press seam allowance over freezer paper.

4. Position the prepared appliqués in place. You can pin them, or iron them to adhere the freezer paper to the background if you prefer.

5. Stitch the appliqués in place (see page 67 for stitching pointers). You can stitch most of the way around a shape, and then lift the edge to remove the paper before continuing, or stitch completely around the shape, and then slit the background fabric to remove the freezer paper from the back of the work.

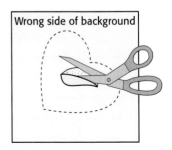

66

Interfacing Method

Using a lightweight, nonwoven, nonfusible interfacing is another option you have for preparing machine appliqué pieces. Like freezer paper, the interfacing acts as a stabilizer when you stitch the pieces in place. However, unlike freezer paper, the interfacing will remain in your quilt, adding a lightweight layer between the background fabric and the appliqués. This adds a little more loft to the shapes, giving them some body, whereas with fusible appliqué the shapes are completely flat against the background fabric.

1. Draw or trace the appliqué shapes onto the interfacing. Cut the shapes out roughly ¼" from all the edges.
2. Place the interfacing on the right side of your appliqué fabric and pin in place.
3. Set your sewing machine to a slightly shorter-than-normal stitch length. Stitch all the way around the shape, sewing exactly on the drawn lines.

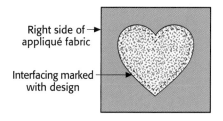

Right side of → appliqué fabric

Interfacing marked → with design

4. Trim around both layers of fabric, leaving a scant ¼" seam allowance. Clip any inner points and blunt any outer ones. Make a slit in the interfacing (be careful not to cut into the fabric!) and turn the shape right side out. Use a bodkin or knitting needle to help you smooth out curves and make the points crisp. Press the shape.
5. Position the appliqué pieces as desired and pin them in place. Then stitch around them, referring to "Stitching Appliqué by Machine," below.

Stitching Appliqué by Machine

Once again, you have a few choices to review and decisions to make. You can use matching threads and satin stitch the pieces in place. You can use contrasting thread to blanket stitch the pieces. Or you can use transparent thread (monofilament) and a blind stitch or narrow zigzag stitch to more closely resemble the look of hand appliqué.

In addition to thread, you'll need to use some sort of a stabilizer beneath your background fabric to ensure that the stitches will form evenly. Otherwise, the needle will move from stitching through one layer of background fabric to multiple layers of appliqué; to freezer paper, fusible web, or interfacing; and then back again to the background fabric.

Stabilizer comes in a variety of forms. Some are ironed in place while others need to be pinned or basted. Some tear away while others must be soaked for removal. Typing paper, tissue paper, or papers that you use for foundation piecing also work. Anything you can sew through that will help prevent the base fabric from shifting as you stitch will improve your machine appliqué stitches.

1. Use an open-toe presser foot (see page 38), a blind-hem foot, or a decorative-stitch foot. The object is for you to be able to see the needle without the foot obscuring your view. Make sure you don't use your ¼" patchwork foot, since that won't allow you to use a zigzag or other wider stitch on your machine without breaking the needle.

2. Set your machine to the desired stitch and thread the machine. For satin stitch, a lightweight (60-weight embroidery) thread is a good option. Use the same thread or one that matches the background fabric in the bobbin. If you're using monofilament, you should use lightweight cotton thread in the bobbin. For blanket stitching, you'll want to use a heavier thread so that it looks more like hand stitching; 40-weight quilting thread works well. Again, use a lightweight cotton thread in the bobbin. And always be sure to use a warm iron when pressing monofilament thread. Anything hotter could melt the thread!

❧ EVEN TENSION ❧

If you're using two different thread weights, you may need to adjust the needle tension to get a nice stitch. Make a sample to practice stitching before you work on your project. If you notice that the bobbin thread is pulling up at the corners of your zigzag or blanket stitch, adjust the top tension and *not* the bobbin. Most machine manufacturers suggest that you don't adjust the bobbin tension.

That said, the bobbin case on some machines has a special eye on the lever that lets you increase the tension without turning the bobbin-case screw. Try threading the bobbin thread through this eye and do a test swatch. You may like the appearance of the stitching with this little bit of added tension.

Stitching Points and Curves

Stitching on the straightaway generally isn't a problem. But tight spots like inner corners, outer points, and curves can be a little trickier.

Outer Points. As you near a narrow outer point, such as a flower petal or leaf point, you'll notice that the stitches will overlap one another when you turn the corner and sew the second side of the point, even if you're using a stitch width that is narrower than usual. It takes a little practice, but you can learn to gradually adjust to a narrower stitch width as you approach an outer corner. At the point, stop with the needle outside of the appliqué, lift the presser foot, and pivot the fabric. Lower the foot and resume stitching, gradually increasing the stitch width back to your original stitch width as you sew. This is most critical with satin stitch.

For blind stitch and blanket stitch, stop with the needle outside of the appliqué shape, turn the fabric so that the needle swings into the appliqué, and take a stitch into the point. Then pivot the fabric so that you're ready to stitch the second side of the point.

Inner Points. The inside point on a heart is a good place to practice this technique. As you approach the inner corner, gradually shorten the stitch length. Then pivot at the corner and gradually increase the stitch length back to your original setting as you continue stitching. This works great with satin stitch.

For blind stitch and blanket stitch, sew slowly and try to adjust your stitch spacing so that you can pivot and take a stitch directly into the inner-point area. Pivot again and continue stitching.

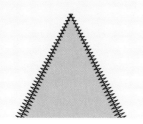

Use a narrower zigzag at point.

Take stitch directly
into inner point.

Curves. As with inner points, you may find that it's helpful to decrease the stitch length for a few stitches when stitching a tight inner curve. This will make neat and tidy satin stitches in a small area. Adjust the stitch length back to your original length and continue stitching. For both inner and outer curves, and for any type of stitch (satin, blanket, or blind stitch), you'll need to pivot every few stitches to keep a smooth curve. The tighter the curve, the more frequently you'll need to pivot.

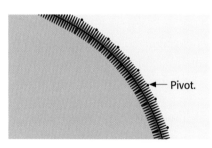

Pivot when needle is outside of the appliqué shape.

Bias Stems by Machine

Just as in hand appliqué, bias stems are strips of fabric cut on the bias so that they can be manipulated into gentle curves to form stems, vines, and basket handles. While for hand appliqué they are commonly made using bias bars (see page 62), for machine stitching you can make them easily without the aid of bias bars.

1. Cut bias strips that are four times the width of your finished vines or stems. For instance, if you want ¼"-wide vines, cut 1"-wide strips.
2. Fold the strips in half lengthwise with right sides together and press.
3. Mark the stem placement on the backing fabric with a pencil, chalk pencil, or chalk wheel. This line will mark the placement of one edge of the stem—not the center line—so mark accordingly.

4. Place the bias strip with the raw edges along the marked line. Pin or baste in place. Put pins with their heads toward you so that you can easily remove them as you sew.

Marked line

Pin vine in place.

5. Using your ¼" presser foot as a guide, stitch ¼" away from the raw edges. Trim the raw edges to roughly ⅛" wide, taking care not to cut the background fabric.

6. Fold the folded edge of the bias strip over the stitching line. Change the presser foot to an open-toe foot and machine stitch the loose edge in place to match your other appliqué. You can use a satin stitch, a blind stitch, blanket stitch, or even a straight stitch if you so desire. If you use a satin stitch or a blanket stitch, go back and stitch along the other edge so that the stem will look balanced.

Fold and stitch.

STITCH GUIDELINES

Stitches vary from one make or model of sewing machine to another, so test the stitching on a practice appliqué to see what settings work best for your machine. Here are some general guidelines for each type of machine appliqué stitch.

Satin Stitch. Set the machine for a narrow zigzag stitch and a shorter-than-normal stitch length. If you make the zigzag stitches too close together, they will produce a ridge of stitching that can look too dense and detract from the appliqué fabrics. Your presser foot may also get hung up on the stitching if it is raised too much. Aim for stitches that are not too open but that don't form so tightly that they overlap.

Satin Stitch

Blind Stitch. If your machine has a blind-stitch setting, you may use it and transparent nylon thread to make your stitching practically invisible. Sew around the shape so that the straight part of the blind stitch runs just outside the edge of the appliqué, into the background fabric only. The "bite" of the blind stitch should swing into the appliqué to hold it in place. Set your machine for a short stitch length and narrow zigzag width.

Blind Stitch

Blanket Stitch. For a folk-art look, try blanket stitching by machine. It looks like half of a ladder, and the thread will be quite visible. Like the blind stitch, the straight part of the stitch should be just outside the edge of the appliqué, and the rungs of the ladder should bite into the appliqué shape. Set your machine so that the stitches are even in length and width.

Blanket Stitch

CHAPTER 8

QUILT SETTINGS

A QUILT SETTING IS THE WAY INDIVIDUAL BLOCKS
ARE ARRANGED TO MAKE A QUILT TOP. BLOCKS
CAN BE SET TOGETHER SIDE BY SIDE, SEPARATED BY
SASHING OR ALTERNATE BLOCKS, TURNED ON
POINT, OR ARRANGED IN A MEDALLION. SOME
TRADITIONAL QUILT BLOCKS REQUIRE A PARTICULAR
SETTING IN ORDER FOR THE OVERALL DESIGN TO BE
APPARENT. OTHER BLOCK DESIGNS PROVIDE
NUMEROUS SETTING OPTIONS.

Simple Straight Sets

In this traditional setting, blocks are set side by side. The blocks are sewn into rows, and then the rows are sewn together.

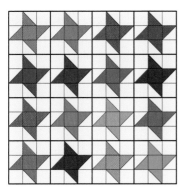

Straight-Set Friendship Star Blocks

Here are some ideas to consider when working with a straight set.

- You can alternate the main pieced or appliquéd block with plain blocks. This is an easy way to expand the size of your finished quilt without having to stitch more blocks.
- You can alternate two different pieced blocks, which can make the quilt more interesting. Sometimes joining two different blocks makes a new overall design appear. These blocks are sometimes called connector or linking blocks. See page 76 for using the

Snowball block and Chain block as linking blocks. They give great results with very little effort!

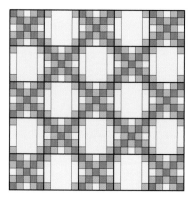

Irish Chain is a two-block design.

- Using the same fabric for the plain blocks as you used for the background of the pieced blocks will make the design blocks appear to float on the surface of the quilt.
- Secondary designs may become prominent at the intersections of the blocks. Blocks with strong

diagonal elements are often good candidates for this look.

Notice the secondary pattern that emerges with straight-set Pinwheel blocks.

Conversely, sometimes blocks set together side by side can look too busy or clunky. Separating them with sashing (or a plain alternate block) may be a better choice.

- Simple straight sets are most effective if the four corner blocks are all the same design. For example, if you are alternating a design block with a plain block, aim for all four corner blocks to be either plain or the same pieced or appliquéd design. This requires an odd number of rows and an odd number of blocks in each row. If the corners don't match, the quilt will appear unbalanced.

• Blocks such as Log Cabin that are divided diagonally into light halves and dark halves can be rotated for a variety of interesting results.

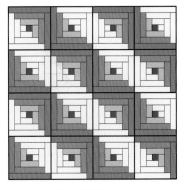

Straight Furrows

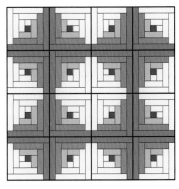

Light and Dark

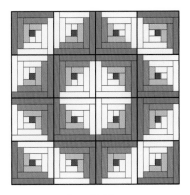

Barn Raising

ADDING COLOR INTEREST TO STRAIGHT SETTINGS

Even if you're working with one particular block and a straight setting, there are ways to enliven the quilt and make it uniquely yours by changing the background color of some blocks and arranging them in a particular way. Here are a few suggestions:

• Make the center of the quilt light and radiate darker as you move toward the outer edge.

• Make the top of the quilt light and gradate to darker as you move toward the bottom.

• Make the upper-left corner light and gradate to darker as you move diagonally toward the bottom right corner.

Simple Connector Blocks

Some blocks, such as a Chain block or a Snowball block, are handy to have in your repertoire. Alternate one of these easy blocks with a block of your choice for amazing results. When the corners of these blocks come together with the corners of the main pieced block, the overall design extends beyond the individual block boundaries.

Snowball Block   Chain Block

Easy Snowball Block

You can easily make a Snowball block in any size to coordinate with the main blocks in your quilt.

1. Measure the size of your main blocks, including the outer seam allowances. Cut the background squares for the Snowball blocks to this size. For instance, if your pieced blocks finish at 9", they measure 9½" with the outer seam allowances. Cut a 9½" square from your background fabric for each Snowball block needed.

2. Measure the size of the corner unit in your main blocks that you want the triangle corner of the Snowball block to line up with. Make sure you allow for a ¼" seam allowance on all sides.

3" finished +
¼" + ¼" seam allowances = 3½"

3. Cut a strip of the Snowball corner fabric the same width as the unit you just measured. For example, if the patch you measured was 3½" x 3½", cut a 3½"-wide strip. Cut the strip into squares. You'll need four squares for each Snowball block.

4. Draw a diagonal line from corner to corner on the wrong side of each square.

5. Place the small squares on the corners of the main snowball square, positioning the diagonal lines as shown. Sew on the line of each of the small squares.

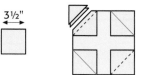

3½"

6. Trim the seams of the small squares to ¼". Press the seam allowance toward the resulting triangles and make sure the block is square before you trim away the excess fabric of the main part of the block.

Snowball Connector
Block

Easy Chain Block

A Chain block will take a little bit longer to construct than a Snowball block, but the sewing is just as simple. This block is made in the fashion of a basic Nine Patch block, but instead of plain squares in the corners, four-patch units are featured.

1. Measure your main blocks for the quilt. Your Chain blocks will need to be the same size as the main blocks. Divide the finished block size (block size minus the outer seam allowances) by three. This will give you the finished size needed for the individual parts of the Nine Patch. For instance, in our example above, if the main patchwork blocks are 9" square, then the units for the Chain block will need to be 3" finished.

2. Using the dimension you calculated above, cut four background squares and one center square for each Chain block. In our example, these squares will all measure 3½" x 3½" (3" plus ½" for seam allowances).

3. For the four-patch corner units, calculate the size needed by dividing the finished unit size in half. In this case, 3" ÷ 2 = 1½". Adding the seam allowances to this measurement yields 2" squares. Cut eight 2" squares of background fabric and eight 2" squares of the fabric you want to use for the chain effect. Sew the 2" squares together into four-patch units as shown.

Four-Patch Unit

4. Lay out the pieces for each block, paying careful attention to the direction of the chain fabric. Sew the units together as you would a Nine Patch block, joining the patches in three rows and then sewing the rows together. Repeat for each block needed.

Chain Connector
Block

More Alternate Block Options

An easy way to give a straight set the look of a diagonal one is to use large triangle squares or Hourglass blocks as alternate blocks. By careful placement of light and dark triangles, the eye will travel along the diagonal lines made by these triangle blocks. The effect is beautiful, and if your main blocks are fairly simple, this option will make your quilt much more interesting than if you'd used plain setting squares.

Triangle-Square Block

Hourglass Block

Triangle Square

For this option, take the *finished size* of your main blocks, add 7/8" for seam allowances, and cut squares to this size from each of two contrasting fabrics. Cut the squares in half diagonally and sew them together in pairs of contrasting fabrics. When you place the triangle squares in your quilt layout, be sure to rotate the blocks so that they form diagonal bands of light and dark. Notice that to achieve

the diagonal effect not all of the triangle squares are positioned in the same direction.

Hourglass

Hourglass blocks are made from four triangles—two each from contrasting fabrics. When used as alternate blocks, the contrasting fabrics seem to frame the blocks and make them look as if they are set on point. Take the finished size of your main blocks, add 1¼" for seam allowances, and then cut squares of this size from each fabric. Cut the squares in half diagonally in each direction to yield four triangles per square. Sew the triangles together to form a square, with opposite sides being the same color. When placing the blocks in the quilt setting, notice that in one row the dark triangles are on the sides of the blocks, while in the next row the dark triangles are at the top and bottom of the blocks.

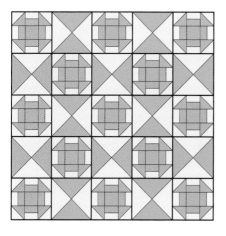

Diagonal Sets

In this arrangement, the blocks are rotated 45° so that they form diagonal rows rather than horizontal rows. A diagonal quilt setting is also commonly called an on-point setting. Some blocks are naturals for this type of setting, such as many of the Basket blocks. When put into straight settings, Basket blocks look a little cockeyed! Other blocks work equally well set on point or in a straight set, such as a Nine Patch or many different Star

blocks. Try your blocks laid out both ways to see which arrangement best suits them.

Diagonal-Set Basket Blocks

Here are a few things you should keep in mind when planning diagonal sets:

- When calculating how big your quilt will be, first multiply the size of the finished block by 1.414. For example, a 16" block x 1.414 = 22.624". This gives you the diagonal measurement of the block. Then multiply the diagonal measurement (in our example, 22.624") by the number of blocks per row to determine the finished quilt size.
- When you lay out the blocks on point, you'll notice that they create a jagged or zigzag edge around the perimeter of your setting. These areas need to be filled in with setting triangles. Side set-

79

ting triangles fill in the side, top, and bottom edges. They are cut with the straight of grain on the longest edge of the triangle. Corner setting triangles are cut with the straight of grain on the short sides. This way, all outer edges of the quilt will be on the straight of grain, rather than on the stretchy bias. For more on cutting setting triangles, see "Side Setting Triangles" at right and "Corner Setting Triangles" on page 81.

- Sew the blocks together in diagonal rows, following the diagram below. Notice how some rows will be longer than others, so take care not to get them out of order. Add the corner triangles last.

- Some quilters like to cut the setting triangles oversized and square up the quilt top after all the rows have been assembled. When trimming, just be sure that you allow for the ¼" seam allowance where the blocks and triangles intersect at the quilt edges.

Side Setting Triangles

We mentioned above that side setting triangles should have the straight of grain along the longest edge so that the outer edges of your quilt won't stretch. The easiest way to cut these triangles is to start with large squares and cut them diagonally in both directions. Each square will yield four setting triangles.

To determine what size square to start with, multiply your block size by 1.414 and add 1¼" to the result for seam allowances. In our 16" block example, the result would be 16" x 1.414 = 22.624" + 1.25" = 23.874" or 23⅞". You can round this up to 24" to give you a little extra leeway in attaching the triangles. The chart on page 133 gives triangle sizes for many sizes of quilt blocks.

**Straight Grain for
Side Setting Triangles**

Corner Setting Triangles

The corner triangles need to have the straight of grain on the two short edges. These triangles are half the size of a finished block and the long side of the corner triangle is the same measurement as the sides of the quilt block. To figure out what size squares to start with, *divide* the width of the quilt block by 1.414 and add ⅞" (.875") for seam allowances. In our example, a 16" block divided by 1.414 = 11.315" + .875" = 12.19" (round to 12¼"). Cut two squares to this measurement, and then cut them in half diagonally to yield a triangle for each corner of your quilt. (For a list of common block sizes and the size squares to cut for corner triangles, see the chart on page 133.)

Straight Grain for
Corner Setting Triangles

≫ ROUNDING ≪ DECIMALS

When you're calculating the size of setting triangles, it's common to get a number that's not easy to cut with a ruler marked in ⅛" increments. Before deciding whether to round up or down, do the entire equation and then decide how to round off.

In our example, we figured that a 16" block divided by 1.414 = 11.315". This could be rounded down to 11.25" or up to 11.5". But since we also needed to add a seam allowance, we finished the equation by adding .875" (⅞") to get 12.19". Common sense tells you to round this off to 12.25". Any excess that is left after sewing can be trimmed away after the entire quilt top is sewn.

Squaring Up the Quilt Top

Working with oversized setting triangles will make it necessary to trim the quilt edges to make them even and give you a uniform ¼" seam allowance around the perimeter of the quilt. Use a 24"-long rotary-cutting ruler and your rotary cutter to trim irregular edges, making sure to leave a ¼" seam allowance all around.

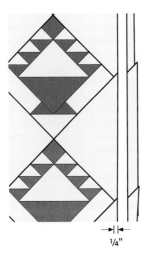

¼"

Sashing

Whether you plan to use a straight set or diagonal set for your quilt, you can add an additional element to your design by incorporating sashing. Sashing is made up of strips of fabric, plain or pieced, that are sewn between blocks to separate them. Sashing is a good option when you have blocks that aren't all quite the same size, when blocks have many seam intersections along their outer edges that would need to be matched and aligned, or when setting blocks side by side simply makes the design look muddled. Sashing separates the blocks, giving a visual break between them. Here are a few other things to keep in mind about sashing:

- If you don't want to add another element to the design, yet you want to separate the pieced blocks (suppose you don't relish matching star points from block to block), consider using the block background fabric for the sashing. The blocks will seem to float on the background, and you've achieved your goal of not having to match dozens of points when you sew the blocks together.

- Sashing can become a unifying factor in a very scrappy quilt, helping to calm down the large mix of fabrics. Just remember that whatever color you choose for the sashing is the color the quilt will become. Even if you use dozens of fabrics in every color of the rainbow, the sashing will be the one constant fabric that sets the tone for your quilt.

- Sashing can be scrappy. For instance, if you want to use red sashing, you can cut strips from a variety of red prints. You will still have the overall look of a red sashing but it will appear more interesting.

- Sashing can be pieced. While it's easiest to cut plain strips of fabric, you can use multiple strips, checkerboard squares, or any other design for sashing.
- Sashing can be uniform, with nothing but strips separating the blocks, or you can use sashing squares (also called cornerstones) to separate the sashing strips at the block corners. While this involves another step, the seam intersections let you easily line up the sashing and blocks in even rows.
- A popular guideline for determining sashing width is to make it one-quarter the size of your finished blocks. Of course, this isn't a hard-and-fast rule, so try cutting a few different widths and auditioning them on your design wall.

Simple Sashing for Straight Sets

1. Cut the sashing fabric into strips of your desired width plus ½" for seam allowances. Measure your blocks. They may not all be the exact same size, but take an average or use the size of the majority of blocks. Then cut the strips into pieces the same length as your average block size. You'll need enough pieces to go between the blocks in vertical rows. For instance, if you have five blocks per row, you'll need four sashing strips per row.

2. Sew a sashing strip between all the blocks in the row. Press the seam allowances toward the sashing strips. Repeat for all vertical rows.

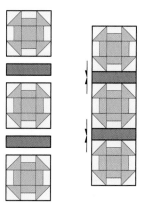

3. Measure the length of each row. If the lengths vary, take the average length and cut long sashing strips to this length. You'll need one more strip than the number of block rows. If the length is greater than 42", you'll either need to piece strips together to make them long enough or cut the strips lengthwise from your fabric, thereby eliminating the need for a seam.

4. Before sewing the sashing and block rows together, it's a good idea to mark the block placement on the sashing strips. Otherwise, it's common for the blocks to not line up horizontally in your finished quilt. To mark the sashing, use pins or make a pencil mark in the seam allowance. At each end, measure

off the distance of one block, including one ¼" seam allowance. Place a pin or draw a hash mark. Then mark off the width of the sashing strip, followed by a quilt block, and so on, until the entire strip has been marked. Make corresponding marks on both sides of each sashing strip so that you can match the seam intersections of the block-sashing rows with the marks on the long sashing strips.

5. Sew the rows together, easing if necessary. Press the seam allowances toward the sashing strips.

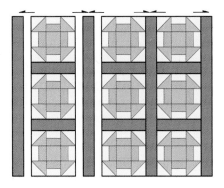

6. Measure the width of the quilt top and cut two sashing strips to this length for the top and bottom of the quilt. Sew them

to the quilt and press the seam allowances toward the sashing strips.

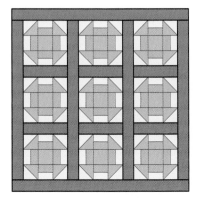

Sashing with Cornerstones

Although this setting looks a bit more complicated than simple sashing, it is actually easier to calculate dimensions for and to sew, since all the sashing strips are the same length. The cornerstones, or sashing squares, are added to the intersections of the sashing strips.

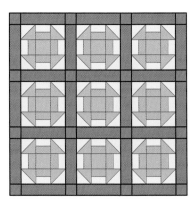

Sashing with Cornerstones

1. Measure your quilt blocks. If they are not all the same size, you can take either the average or the most common measurement of the group. Cut the sashing strips the same length as the unfinished block.

2. For the cornerstones, cut strips the same width as the sashing strips, and then cut them into squares. If your sashing is cut 3½" wide, then cut the cornerstones 3½" x 3½".

3. Sew the sashing strips to the top and bottom of the first block in each row. Then sew the sashing strips to the bottoms only of the remaining blocks. Press all seam allowances toward the sashing. Join the blocks into vertical rows.

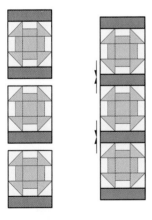

4. Make the sashing rows by sewing a cornerstone to each end of the first sashing strip in the row and to one end of all the remaining sashing pieces. Sew the sashing pieces together into vertical rows, pressing the seam allowances toward the sashing.

Sashing Row

5. Sew the sashing and block rows together, matching the seam intersections. Press the seam allowances toward the sashing rows.

Sashing for Diagonal Sets

Simple sashing for a diagonal set makes an interesting lattice weave design, while adding cornerstones makes planning and sewing the sashing easier, just as for straight sets. Whether you use cornerstones or not, the important thing to know about diagonal settings is that you will need to calculate the size of the setting triangles based on the block size plus sashing width, not just the block size. If you don't account for the sashing, it will be an expensive lesson; your setting triangles will be too small and you'll have to start over with new fabric.

Diagonal Set with Sashing

1. Determine how wide you want your sashing to be and cut strips to that width. From the strips, cut short sashing strips that are the same length as your block. Cut one short sashing strip for each block, plus one more for each diagonal row and two more for corners. For example, if you have 13 blocks set in five diagonal rows as in the Basket quilt shown on page 79, you'd need 20 sashing strips: 13 + 5 + 2 = 20.

2. Sew a short sashing strip to the left side of each block. Take care not to rotate directional blocks such as Basket blocks.

3. Lay out the blocks in rows. Sew the block-sashing strip units together into rows. Add another sashing strip to the right end of each row, including the single-block corner rows.

4. Cut two sashing strips, one for the top of the upper left-corner block and one for the lower right-corner block. These strips need to be the width of the finished block, plus two times the finished width of the sashing, plus ½" for seam allowances. Sew the strips to the blocks and

press all seam allowances toward the sashing strips.

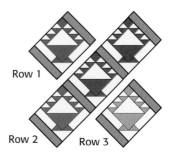

Row 1

Row 2 Row 3

5. Calculate the size needed for the side setting triangles. Add the finished size of your block to the finished width of your sashing. Multiply the result by 1.414 and then add 1¼" for seam allowances. For example, if the blocks in your quilt are 8" finished and your sashing will finish at 2" wide, your calculation will look like this: 8" + 2" = 10" x 1.414 = 14.14 + 1.25" = 15.39". Round up the result to 15½". Cut squares to this size, and then cut them twice diagonally to yield four side setting triangles each.

6. For corner triangles, base the calculation on the finished block size plus two times the width of the finished sashing. Divide the result by 1.414 and add ⅞" for seam allowances, as follows. 8" + 2" + 2" = 12" ÷ 1.414 = 8.49" + .875" = 9.36". Round the result up to 9½". Cut two squares to this size, and then cut each one in half once diagonally to yield four corner triangles.

7. Measure the block rows to determine how long you need to cut the long sashing strips. Excluding the single-block rows, you'll need a sashing strip for the top of each row, as well as for the bottom of the last row. Some of your rows may require strips longer than 42", so you'll either need to piece strips together to get the required length or cut them on the lengthwise grain to avoid seaming.

Note: The sashing strips will need to be trimmed diagonally at each end. Do this after assembling the rows.

8. Measure and mark the sashing strips as in step 4 of "Simple Sashing for Straight Sets" on page 83. The markings will help you keep the blocks aligned from one row to another.

9. Sew the sashing to the top of each block row and press the seam allowances toward the sashing. Then sew a side setting triangle to the ends of each row. Again, press the seam allowances toward the sashing.

10. Sew the rows together and attach the final corner triangles. Press as before.

❧ ADDING ❧ CORNERSTONES TO DIAGONAL SETS

While adding cornerstones creates extra pieces for your quilt layout, as in straight settings, it also makes the sashing easier to calculate and to match as you sew. The sashing is all cut into the shorter block lengths, so you don't need to worry about cutting it on the lengthwise grain. However, you still need to calculate your setting triangle sizes as described in step 4 of "Sashing for Diagonal Sets," taking care to allow for the width of the sashing as well as the block size. If you like the look that cornerstones give, this will be the simpler way to assemble a diagonal quilt with sashing.

Framing Blocks

Framing blocks, also known as adding coping strips, is similar to adding sashing in that strips of fabric separate the blocks in a quilt. However, instead of a single strip of fabric between the block rows, each block is framed individually.

Why would you use framing strips? They're a great way to make assorted blocks a uniform size so that you can assemble a quilt top easily. If you've ever participated in a block swap, you've seen first hand how much variation there can be in ¼" seam allowances. If you have a set of blocks that vary in size from 10¼" to 10¾", adding framing or coping strips around each block will enable you to trim each block to a standard size.

Another use for framing strips is to float your blocks. Suppose you're planning to set your blocks side by side with an alternate block, but it will involve lots of seam intersections. By adding framing strips that match the block background fabric, the blocks will appear to float on the background, and you'll have just straight pieces of fabric to sew together rather than points and intersections.

Framing strips are also handy if you have two different sizes of blocks, such as a 10" Chain block and a 9" Star block. Add ½" finished framing strips around the stars, and now all your blocks will be 10" finished. The stars will float on the background fabric between the Chain blocks.

Framed blocks can be set together in any way you desire. You can still add sashing and cornerstones, or try an Attic Windows effect by framing two adjacent sides of the block in a light-color fabric and the other two sides in a dark fabric, mitering the corners as you go. (See "Fold and Stitch Mitered Corners" on page 98 for details.)

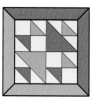

Attic Windows Framing

Bar Sets

Beauty often comes from simplicity. Vertical rows of blocks alternating with strips of fabric creates a bar setting. The blocks themselves may be sewn together in straight-set rows, or they may be turned on point. For blocks set on point, you'll need to straighten the edges of the rows with setting triangles. The sizes are calculated just as for a diagonal set, or you can refer to the chart on page 133 and look up the size you need for your block size.

The bars may be single strips of fabric, composed of several different strips of fabric sewn together, or even a patchwork strip such as the Flying Geese bars, shown right. A wide center strip flanked by narrower ones on each side is a common option.

Amish quiltmakers often use a pattern called Bars, which is simply a number of vertical solid fabric bars sewn together. These quilts typically have a wide border, sometimes with corner squares, and intricate quilting, such as cables or feathers in the bars.

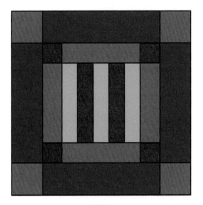

Amish Bars

Bars Made of Flying Geese Units

Bars Made of Large-Scale Print Fabric

Zigzag Sets

A zigzag setting is a relatively easy way to turn a set of ordinary quilt blocks into a quilt that's full of drama and movement. Although a zigzag setting looks complicated, it's really quite easy to do. All you need is your set of blocks and the fabric that you want to use for the zigzag. From this fabric, you'll cut setting triangles, just as you would for a diagonal quilt setting. The setting triangles are sewn to the blocks to put them on point and give them a straight vertical edge. To distinguish this from the straight bar set, the blocks are then offset or staggered from one row to the next by using half blocks.

Keep in mind that you don't have to use all one fabric for the zigzag. As long as the color you choose, either light or dark, provides enough contrast with the quilt blocks, you can use a variety of fabrics in one color to make a scrappy zigzag setting.

Zigzag settings need to have an odd number of rows for the quilt to look balanced, or symmetrical. In the first example, the two outside rows are composed of full blocks. The inside row of the quilt alternates between half blocks, on the top and bottom, and full blocks.

In the second example, each row is composed of full blocks and one half block. The rows alternate between the half block being on the top and on the bottom.

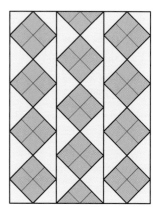

Example 1

Example 2

❧ HALF BLOCKS ❧

When making half blocks for the rows that require them, remember that a ¼" seam allowance is needed on the outside edge. This means that you can't just make a full block and cut it in half diagonally to yield two half blocks, or your half blocks will come up short.

You'll either need to draft the half block so that seam allowances are included along the longest edge of the block, or try this easy solution: use plain setting triangles instead. Cut additional setting triangles from the same fabric as the other zigzag triangles and place them in the quilt layout where the half blocks would have been. This gives you a bigger area for some fancy quilting!

**Plain Half Blocks in
Center Column**

Medallion Sets

Medallion quilts use one or more blocks—pieced or appliquéd—to create a central design or focal point. This center design, which can be set straight or on point, is then framed by other quilt elements, such as sashing, setting triangles, pieced blocks, appliquéd motifs, or borders. Framing the center block or blocks with the same fabric used in the background of the center portion makes the central design appear to float above the other parts of the quilt.

Straight-Set Medallion

On-Point Medallion

When planning an on-point medallion design, use the handy corner setting triangle formula (see page 133) for calculating the size you need to make the setting triangles. This doesn't mean that you can only use large, plain triangles in the design, but figuring the overall size needed will help in planning how to divide the corner triangle areas into smaller units.

For example, if you have a center medallion that measures 24" square and you want to set it on point, divide 24" by 1.414. This will give you the finished size of each setting triangle, which is 17". You could cut squares 17⅞" (remember to add seam allowances!) and then cut the squares in half to form corner triangles. Or you could cut smaller triangles and frame them attic-

window style as described on page 88. Another option would be to divide the 17" in half and make a series of smaller triangles to fill in the large space as shown below. The options are really limitless; use graph paper or a computer drafting program and get creative.

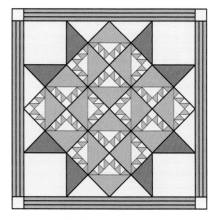

Divide large corner setting triangles into smaller units such as the star points shown here.

CHAPTER 9

BORDERS

THE BORDER IS THE FRAME FOR YOUR MASTER-PIECE. SOME QUILTS NEED NO FRAME, WHILE OTHERS CERTAINLY BENEFIT FROM ONE OR MORE BORDERS.

Simple borders can be a single strip of fabric or multiple strips. Pieced borders are often alternated with plain ones, and the combination can be quite effective. Appliqué borders are another option. They look nice combined with narrower plain or pieced borders on appliqué quilts. Appliqué in the border can add a nice touch to a pieced quilt, too, adding some softness to the sharp angles and straight lines of traditional patchwork.

Choosing a Border Style

If you're following a printed quilt pattern, perhaps you decided on the border treatment before you began your quilt. Or maybe you designed your own quilt on graph paper or your computer, right down to the last border detail. Even so, it may still be a good idea to audition border options after the interior of the quilt top has been pieced or appliquéd. Seeing fabric options in person may help you decide on the best option for your quilt. Here are a few pointers for selecting a border:

- The width of the border is a crucial factor in how the finished quilt will look. When using multiple borders, the first border is usually the narrowest, and the outer border is usually the widest. Most often the outer border is the darkest color. Dark colors provide a stopping place and tell the eye where the boundary is. Multiple borders are usually made up of different widths because that gives a more pleasing effect.
- To help you determine what width of borders to use, cut strips from your border possibilities and hang them on your design wall or lay them on the floor beside the quilt top to see how the fabric will look and what proportion works best.

No Border

Double Border

Pieced Border

Appliqué Border

- If you have leftover blocks or units from your quilt top, try placing those next to your quilt to see if they might work for a border treatment. Perhaps turning them on point or separating them from the main quilt with a narrow border will set off your quilt top perfectly.

- Look through quilt books and magazines for ideas. The most common approach to borders may be to use one or more plain borders, but looking at what other quiltmakers have done may spark a solution for your border that otherwise might not have occurred to you.

⁓ A CLUE ⁓
FROM THE PAST

Have you ever noticed that many antique quilts don't have borders, or that the borders are irregular, with sides that are not all alike? Often quiltmakers of the past didn't have access to new yardage, so quilts were simply made of scraps. If you want to replicate this look on a new quilt, leave the border off and simply audition binding fabrics for your quilt.

Cutting Border Strips

It is important to construct the border correctly, as this will make the quilt hang straight. If you attach border strips to the sides of your quilt and then trim off the excess fabric to fit, you can easily end up with a quilt that's lopsided or has a wavy or rippled border. It's best to measure and cut borders to fit precisely.

1. Use a square ruler to check each corner to make sure that it is perfectly square. You might need to shave away a bit of fabric to square them up. Also trim any excess fabric from setting triangles to make sure that your quilt top edges are straight and true.

2. Measure the length and width of your quilt top. Don't just measure the edges, since they are more likely to become stretched out of shape than the center of the quilt. Measure the center and along each edge. Average the three results to get the dimensions of your quilt top.

3. Cut border strips to the desired width that are long enough to fit your quilt. Strips cut from the lengthwise grain of the fabric will stretch less than those cut from the crosswise grain.

   However, if you do not have enough fabric for cutting lengthwise, crosswise grain works perfectly fine. You may piece strips together to get the necessary length. More specifics about measuring your quilt depending on the type of border you select will be covered in "Butted Corners," "Corner Squares," and "Mitered Corners," which follow.

❦ SEAMING ❦
FABRIC FOR A BORDER

If you do not have a continuous strip of fabric long enough for a border, you may piece strips together. A seam that is at an angle is less noticeable than a straight seam. To do this, place the short ends of the strips at right angles to each other, with right sides facing. Sew from intersection to intersection. Then trim the excess fabric ends, leaving a ¼" seam allowance. Press the seam allowances open.

To make a straight seam, join the short ends of the strips and sew a ¼" seam allowance. Make sure to trim off the selvages before sewing the strips together. Press the seam allowances open. An open seam has less bulk and is less noticeable in a long, unpieced stretch of fabric.

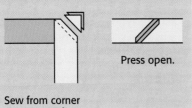

Press open.

Sew from corner to corner. Trim.

Butted Corners

With this type of corner treatment, borders are sewn to two opposite sides of the quilt, and then the remaining borders are attached to the other two sides of the quilt. You can attach either the side borders first or the top and bottom borders first. On rectangular quilts, side borders are often attached before the top and bottom borders, since this order may require less fabric depending on the size of your quilt.

1. For the side strips, measure from top to bottom through the center of the quilt.

2. Cut two border strips the desired width and trim them to the exact length of your measurement from step 1. Sew a border to each side of the quilt. Press the seam allowance toward the borders.

3. For the top and bottom borders, measure across the center of the quilt, including the borders that you've just attached.

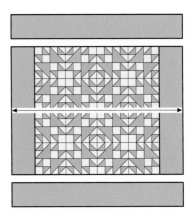

4. Cut two border strips the desired width by the measurement from step 3. Sew the borders to the top and bottom of the quilt. Press the seam allowances toward the borders.

⚓ IRREGULAR ⚓ WIDTH BORDERS

There's no rule that says all borders must be the same width or even cut from the same fabric. If your quilt isn't quite traditional, it may be fun to use a wider bottom border than top border. Or perhaps add top and bottom borders but no side borders, to suit the mood of your quilt. Sometimes it's fun to do the unexpected.

Corner Squares

A simple way to add extra interest to plain butted borders is by adding corner squares. These squares can be plain squares of contrasting fabric, or they can be pieced quilt blocks. The block design can complement the quilt interior, repeat the block design used in the quilt, or use just one component of the block design.

1. Measure both the length and width of the quilt as described, opposite. Cut two borders to each of these measurements in the desired width.

2. Sew the side borders to the sides of the quilt top.

3. Cut four corner squares the same width as your border strips. For example, if your borders are cut 4½" wide (to finish at 4"), then cut four 4½" x 4½" squares. Alternately, you can piece four blocks that measure 4½" with seam allowances.

4. Sew a corner square to each end of the top and bottom quilt borders. Press the seam allowances toward the borders. Sew the finished borders to the top and bottom of the quilt. Press the seam allowances toward the borders.

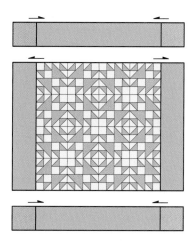

Mitered Corners

Mitered corners look especially beautiful if you use a fabric that can be matched when cut at a 45° angle, such as a striped fabric or a border print. Mitered corners also look nice when you have multiple strip borders. If your quilt blocks are set on point or if your quilt has an otherwise strong diagonal focus in the design, a border with mitered corners may be a good option to frame your quilt.

Measuring for Mitered Borders

A mitered corner requires a little extra fabric so that you will have enough to make the diagonal seam that will join the adjacent borders.

1. Measure the total length of the quilt. Add two times the width of the border plus 5". Cut two strips to this length for the side borders of the quilt.

2. Measure the total width of the quilt. Add two times the width of the border plus 5". Cut two strips to this length for the top and bottom borders of the quilt. For example, imagine that the quilt measures 36" x 40" and the borders are 4" wide. 36" + 4" + 4" + 5" = 49". Cut two pieces of border fabric 49" long. 40" + 4" + 4" + 5" = 53". Cut two pieces of border fabric 53" long.

Fold and Stitch Mitered Corners

The traditional way to stitch a mitered corner involves folding the miter, stitching along the crease, and trimming away excess fabric. That method is explained here. Another method, where the miter cuts are made first, follows on page 100.

1. Sew the side border strips to the quilt, stopping ¼" from the edges of the quilt top. Backstitch at the beginning and end of the seam. Press the seam allowances toward the border.

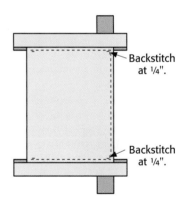

Backstitch at ¼".

Backstitch at ¼".

2. Sew the top and bottom border strips to the quilt in the same way as for the side borders. You now have two tails of border fabric extending from each corner.

3. To create the miter, overlap the two adjoining borders at one corner of the quilt. Fold the top border under at a 45° angle so that it is aligned with the underneath border as shown. Press the fold. Use a square ruler to check that the angle is accurate and the corner of the quilt is square.

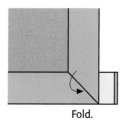

Fold.

4. Place a piece of masking tape over the fold to hold the layers together. Then turn the quilt over and draw a stitching line just outside of the crease.

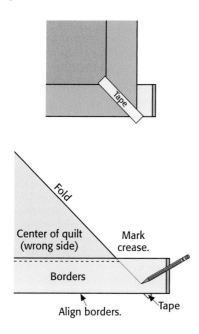

Center of quilt (wrong side)

Mark crease.

Borders

Align borders.

Tape

5. Fold the quilt top right sides together, diagonally from the corner, matching the long edges of the border strips. Sew on the stitching line, starting exactly at the inside corner. Backstitch, taking care not to stitch into the quilt top. Then continue sewing on the line to the outer edge of the borders. Remove the tape and trim the seam allowance to ¼". Press the seam open.

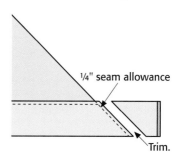

¼" seam allowance

Trim.

⌇ MITERS WITH ⌇ MULTIPLE BORDERS

When using multiple strips for a border, you can sew the strips for each side of the quilt together first and attach them to the sides of the quilt as a unit. Then miter the corners, matching the seam intersections so that each color border will have a perfect miter.

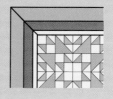

Cut and Sew Mitered Corners

If the folding, taping, pinning, and marking of mitered corners seems like a lot of effort, try this alternate method. You will measure the borders to fit, cut the ends at a 45° angle before attaching them, and simply treat the adjoining corners as set-in seams.

1. Measure the length of your quilt top. Add two times the width of your borders, plus an extra inch for insurance. Cut two border strips to this length for the sides of your quilt.

2. On each strip, mark the length of your quilt top along one edge with a pencil or chalk.

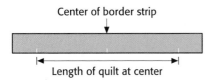

Center of border strip

Length of quilt at center

3. Lay a border strip on your cutting mat, and then place a rotary-cutting ruler over the strip so that the 45° line is aligned with the marked edge of the border, and the edge of the ruler intersects the marking point. Trim off the excess border. Repeat for the opposite end of the border strip, making sure that the corner is angled in the opposite direction, as shown. Then repeat for the other side border.

Cut at 45° angle.

4. Measure the width of the quilt top. Add two times the width of your borders, plus an extra inch for insurance. Cut two strips to this length for the top and bottom borders. Mark and trim as for the side borders.

5. Sew each border strip to the quilt top, matching midpoints and the ends of the borders with the ends of the quilt top. Stop stitching ¼" from each end of the border.

6. At each corner, fold the quilt top in half, right sides together. Align the diagonally cut ends of the border and sew the seam from the inside point to the outer edge. Remember to backstitch at the inner point. Press the seam allowances open.

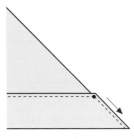

Stitch.

~~ PUCKERED ~~
MITERS?

If you notice that you have a pucker at the inner edge of your mitered corner, it's probably because you took one or two stitches into the quilt top area. An easy fix is to use your seam ripper to remove *just one stitch* at the inside corner. Press again to see if the corner will lie flat. If not, take out one more stitch. Most likely, this is all that is needed to make your miter perfect.

Appliqué Borders

Most traditional appliqué quilts have beautiful borders composed of meandering vines, flowers and leaves, or gracefully curved swags alternating with ribbons, flowers, or some other motif. In order for the quilt to be aesthetically pleasing, the border motifs must be in line with the design blocks. The appliqué designs should also go around the corners in a pleasing manner. This isn't as critical for trailing vines and stems that curve with flowers and leaves as it is for symmetrical designs such as swags, but well-placed flowers will give the border a pleasing balance.

Balance and Symmetry

Let's look at an example of a border composed of curved swags that are intersected with a flower motif. One option is to have the flowers line up with the center of the design blocks and the swags line up with the seam line of two blocks. This makes a symmetrical design that's easy for the eye to follow.

If the same swag design were placed indiscriminately in relation to the design blocks, the whole quilt would have a somewhat unbalanced effect.

Symmetrical Swag Border

Unbalanced Swag Border

Resizing Designs to Fit

There are lots of ways to get a nice-looking border with a minimum amount of math. If you're starting with a pattern that you like but that doesn't quite fit your proportions, you can adapt it.

For example, imagine that you have a swag border design that fits nicely with a 10" block, but your blocks measure 9". To convert the design so that it will work, trace it onto a piece of graph paper. Copy half of a swag (or other motif) at either end. You may have to tape two pieces of graph paper together to accommodate your design.

Fold the paper in half to find the exact middle of the swag, and draw a pencil mark there. Mark ½" from each side of the center point. Now fold the paper, bringing each of the ½" markings to meet the center line. You've just deleted 1" from the swag. The swag lines will be somewhat interrupted, but now you can pencil in new ones that meet gracefully with the original markings.

If your design has two shorter swags with a center motif, then you must adjust the length of the swags so that half of the total you need to reduce is taken from each swag. Corner designs can be adjusted by the same method.

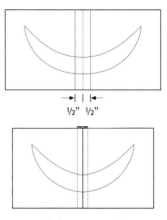

Fold along ½" marking
to shorten design.

You can also make your own appliqué designs. Fold a piece of graph paper and draw half of the motif you wish to use. Go over the pencil lines with a heavy marker, and then trace them onto the other side with the paper still folded. Dinner plates are convenient to use for precise curves. Or draw curving vines freehand, making mirror images with the folded graph-paper technique.

Decide whether you want butted or mitered border corners, and then measure and cut them accordingly (see pages 96–100). Appliqué the designs to the borders before attaching them to the quilt top, but do not work the corners yet. Sew the borders to the quilt, pinning carefully so that the border designs match up with the block designs. Miter or butt the corners, and then complete their appliqué designs.

CHAPTER 10

BACKING AND BATTING

ONCE YOU COMPLETE THE QUILT TOP, IT IS READY
TO BE LAYERED WITH THE TWO OTHER QUILT COM-
PONENTS: BATTING AND BACKING. BATTING IS THE
FLUFFY INNER LAYER THAT IS SANDWICHED
BETWEEN THE BACKING FABRIC AND THE QUILT TOP
TO GIVE IT LOFT AND WARMTH. HAND OR MACHINE
QUILTING STITCHED THROUGH ALL THREE LAYERS
SECURES THEM TOGETHER. QUILT BACKINGS CAN BE
AS PLAIN OR AS FANCY AS YOU'D LIKE.

Backing

Years ago most quilters used a plain
fabric for the backing, often
unbleached muslin because it was
economical and readily available.
Today it's quite common to see all
sorts of colorful quilt backings.
From a printed fabric that coordi-
nates with the front of the quilt to
pieced leftovers from the quilt top
and an artfully pieced second quilt
top, quilt backings can range from
being quite practical to making
your quilt reversible. When planning your backing, keep the following pointers in mind:

• Choose backing fabric that is the
same fiber content as the quilt
top, including thread count. The
higher the thread count, the
harder it is to quilt through. This
means that bed sheets are not a
good choice. They have a very
high thread count.

• Some quilting fabrics come in
wider widths: 60", 90", and even
108". Consider purchasing one of
these fabrics for larger-size quilts,
and you won't have to seam the
backing.

• Plan your backing so that you'll
have at least 3" extra on all sides

if you'll be quilting it yourself. If you plan to have someone else do your quilting, check with him or her to be sure you have the right amount. For example, long-arm machine quilters may ask for up to 6" extra on all sides.

- If you're using just one fabric for the backing (as opposed to making a scrappy leftover backing), determine how best to piece it. Seams can run vertically or horizontally, and sometimes your choice can save you fabric.

Economical Piecing

Most quilting fabric today is roughly 42" wide once you account for shrinkage and removing the selvages. Calculate how much backing fabric you need based on that width.

- Quilts less than 40" wide can use one length of fabric.
- A 72" x 90" (twin-size) quilt will need 5⅓ yards of backing fabric; two lengths with a vertical seam.
- An 81" x 96" (full-size) quilt will need 7¼ yards of backing fabric; three lengths with two horizontal seams.
- A 90" x 108" (queen-size) quilt will need 8 yards of backing fabric; three lengths with two horizontal seams.
- A 120" x 120" (king-size) quilt will need 10½ yards of backing

fabric; three lengths with either two horizontal or two vertical seams.

Twin   Full

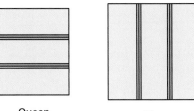

Queen   King

If your quilt size isn't listed above, first add the extra inches needed for a quilting allowance (3" to 6" per quilt) to both the width and length measurements of your quilt. Then divide the width measurement by the width of the backing fabric. Round the result up to the nearest whole number. This result is how many lengths of fabric you need.

Now, multiply the length measurement by the number of fabric lengths you need; divide the result by 36", and that equals the number of yards of fabric you need to buy. For instance, if your quilt is 60" x 80", use the following equation: 60" + 3" + 3" = 66". 66" ÷ 42" = 1.57; round up to 2 for the lengths needed. 80" + 3" + 3"= 86". 86" x 2 lengths = 172". 172" ÷ 36" = 4.78 yards. Buy 4⅞ yards to back this quilt.

Pieced Backing Options

Buying good-quality quilting fabric for a quilt backing can get expensive, especially when you need 10 yards of it! It can also be hard to find just the right fabric with enough yards on the bolt for you to make your backing. There are other options.

If you have a stash of fabric, try using it up. (Don't worry, you'll barely make a dent!) My good friend Donna makes delightful backings by using up fabrics from her shelves. Sometimes she cuts large squares and sews them together, sometimes strips, sometimes a combination. The quilts are a delight, whatever side you're looking at!

Batting

The array of batting available to quilters today is amazing. And, it can be just a little confusing if you're not sure what you like or need. Different fiber contents and the manufacturing processes can lead to different results in your finished quilt. Let's first review the general terms used to describe batting, and then we'll take a look at the specific characteristics of different battings.

Batting Terms

Bearding. When loose fibers from the batting make their way through the quilt top, it's referred to as bearding. Bearding is most noticeable on dark quilts because batting is generally white or off-white. Consider using a dark-colored batting if the quilt top is primarily dark, although only polyester batting is available this way.

If bearding occurs, do not pull the fibers out through the quilt top. This will only exacerbate the problem. Instead, carefully clip the fibers close to the quilt top.

Glazing and Bonding. During these processes, batting is coated on both sides as a means to hold the fibers together and reduce the chance of fiber migration. Glazing and bonding are used on cotton, polyester, and blended battings. Batting that has been treated this way allows you to place quilting stitches at farther intervals and still keep the integrity of the batting.

Loft. The thickness of the batting is referred to as loft. The higher the loft, the thicker the batting and thus the warmer the quilt. Low-loft batting is preferred for hand quilting, while low- or medium-loft batting works well for machine quilting; high-loft or ultra-loft battings are best reserved for tied comforters.

Needlepunching. In this process, barbed needles are punched in and out of the batting, twisting and tangling the fibers together. This process serves the same purpose as glazing and bonding, without adding a coating to the fibers. However, you may find it a little more difficult to quilt through needlepunched battings since they are very dense.

Needling. This term refers to how easy (or difficult) it is to put the quilting needle through the batting. This is an important consideration if you are planning to quilt by hand. Generally, cotton batting is harder to needle than polyester or wool; even then, some types of cotton battings are easier to needle than others.

Scrim. This is a thin layer of polyester that is applied to one side of some battings to help prevent fiber migration. You can find cotton, wool, and polyester battings with a scrim. It lets you quilt farther apart, yet it adds polyester to otherwise natural fiber battings.

Shrinkage. Polyester batting does not shrink. Cotton batting will shrink if washed in warm or hot water and machine dried. If you want your quilt to look antique, use a cotton batting, and machine wash and dry the finished quilt. The batting will shrink slightly, making the fabric pucker slightly at the quilting stitches and giving the quilt a softly worn, antique look.

Quilts with wool batting can be dry-cleaned or hand washed in tepid water, and then air dried. Be sure to read the manufacturer's recommendations for your particular batting before laundering.

Selecting the Right Batting

Batting is available in a variety of fiber contents, including cotton, polyester, wool, and polyester-cotton blends. In this section, we'll review the basic characteristics of each type of fiber, but you should know that even if they're made of the same fiber content, battings can vary from one manufacturer to another. If you're unsure about a particular product, ask at your local quilt shop for recommendations, or see if they'll give you a sample to test before you commit to a bed-size batting.

Low-loft, needlepunched cotton batting (bottom), medium-loft polyester (center), cotton with scrim (top).

106

Before selecting a batting, think about how you plan to use the finished quilt. Will it hang on a wall? If so, stiffer cotton batting may be the best option because it will keep its shape. Is it for snuggling under? A softer, low-loft cotton is a good choice because it will drape better than a higher loft batting, and with repeated washings it will become even softer.

Also consider your climate. Cotton breathes, but it may feel heavy to sleep under. Wool is much less dense than cotton, so it is not as heavy as a cotton batting. It also breathes and keeps you warm. Polyester is lightweight and provides plenty of warmth, but it doesn't breathe like natural fibers do. Here are some more points to consider before buying your next batting:

Cotton. Cotton fibers tend to stick to fabric, which makes cotton a good choice for machine quilting. You'll have less shifting of layers as you guide your quilt under the machine. Hand quilting with cotton batting can be more difficult, so choose a low-loft cotton and one that doesn't have a scrim or bonding; you'll find it's easier to needle. Of course, without a scrim or bonding, you'll need to quilt more closely together so that the cotton fibers won't migrate as your quilt is used and laundered. Note that cotton shrinks when washed, but sometimes this is desirable if you're after a softly worn, antique look.

If you want to use cotton batting but don't want the finished quilt to shrink when washed, you'll need to select a batting that can be prewashed. Check labels carefully. Prewashing is not recommended for all types.

Wool. This is an amazing fiber! Hand quilting through wool is as easy as cutting butter with a hot knife. It is warm and lofty without being too heavy, and it can be fluffed up by airing it out in the open. Because of its loft, wool batting will give your quilt a different appearance than cotton batting. If you want more of an old-fashioned look, choose a wool batting with a low-loft, which is apt to give the quilt more drapability, too. Wool battings are more expensive than other fibers, and if you launder your quilt, you will need to lay it flat to dry. If these factors aren't drawbacks for you, you'll find wool to be quite a durable option.

Polyester. Polyester batting is easy to quilt by hand, and it comes in the widest variety of lofts, from very thin and drapey to extra-high loft that is suitable for tied comforters. It's not, however, the best choice for machine quilting, since the fibers are slippery and tend to shift more easily than natural fiber battings. If you're making a wall hanging, note that polyester batting stretches and may not retain its shape as well as a cotton batting would.

Blends. Depending on your goals, a cotton-polyester blend may be the right option, as this type of batting combines the best qualities of the two fibers. These battings are usually 80% cotton and 20% polyester.

A blend batting gives you the look of cotton but is easier to hand quilt because of the polyester content. And because of the polyester, these battings can also be quilted a little farther apart than those that are 100% cotton.

READ THE LABEL

Batting packages contain lots of important information. They describe how to launder the batting, whether or not it can be or should be prewashed, and how far apart you'll need to quilt. (If you buy batting cut from a large roll, ask the store clerk for information on care and handling.)

The amount of quilting required is an important consideration, as quilts that do not have enough quilting will wear out faster due to the stress and strain on the minimal amount of stitches that were used to hold all the layers together. Some battings, particularly those that don't have a scrim, bonding, or glazing, or those that haven't been needle-punched, require very close quilting—¼" to ½" apart. Other labels may indicate that you can quilt up to 8" apart, but for best results I recommend that your stitching lines be no farther than 3" apart. Your quilt will look nicer and it will be better able to stand the test of time.

CHAPTER 11

QUILTING

It's time to quilt. Now you can turn your quilt top into a usable, dimensional work of art to enjoy. The first thing you need to decide is whether you want to quilt by hand or machine. (Or maybe you'd like to turn the whole thing over to a professional quilter!)

Your decision about a quilting method will guide you when making other decisions along the way, including the best or easiest or fastest way to mark and baste your quilt. In this chapter, you'll find suggestions to help you with these and other common issues that you'll face when you're ready to quilt.

Marking the Quilt Top

For many people, marking a quilt top is an unpleasant task, a necessary evil to go through to get from a quilt top to a completed quilt. It can require a lot of bending over and kneeling, which can make for an aching back and sore knees. With that thought in mind, there are ways around marking or drawing the quilting lines on your quilt top. But there are times when marking can't be avoided. And

when you do need to mark designs, they need to be dark enough to see clearly while you're stitching yet easy to remove when you're done. Over the years, quilters and manufacturers have come up with all sorts of tools and ways to mark quilts, but no particular method is perfect for every situation.

No-Mark Options

Depending on the style of quilting you are doing, the quilt top may need to be marked at some point. But marking doesn't necessarily mean drawing a line on top of your quilt. Here are some ideas for creating a design without drawing actual lines on your quilt that you'll need to wash out later.

Stitch in the ditch. You can do this by hand or machine. Make your quilting stitches right along the seam lines of patchwork or just outside the edges of appliqué shapes. You simply follow the line of the fabric designs; there is no need to mark.

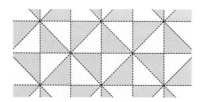

Echo quilting. Rather than following the seam line, echo quilting outlines the appliqué or patchwork shapes. You can simply eyeball the distance from the shape or you can use the width of your presser foot as a guide. Start the first round ⅛" to ¼" away from the motif. You can stitch each consecutive row the same distance apart or make the rows progressively farther apart.

Masking tape. Masking tape is a great way to mark straight lines, such as square or diamond-shaped grids, horizontal or vertical channels, or even outline quilting (done ¼" away from the seam line). Quilt shops carry ¼"-wide quilters' masking tape, but you can also use ½"-, ¾"-, or 1"-wide tape depending on

your desired effect. Place the tape (use your rotary-cutting ruler to help with the angles) and stitch on either side of it. You can reposition the same piece of tape a number of times before it will no longer stick.

❧ STICKY SITUATIONS

Be sure to remove masking tape when you're finished quilting for the day so that you don't leave a sticky residue on your quilt. It's also a good idea to touch a fresh piece of tape to your jeans or other fabric before sticking it to your quilt. This helps reduce its tackiness so that it won't be too sticky on your quilt.

Freezer-paper or Con-Tact templates. An easy way to mark curves or other shapes on your quilt top is to cut the designs out of freezer paper and then use a warm iron to press them onto your quilt top. Clear Con-Tact paper is used in the same way, only it has a self-stick backing and you can see through it for easy positioning. Stitch around the templates by hand or machine, and peel them off when you're finished. You can usually use a shape several times before the stickiness wears off.

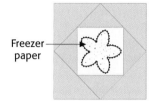

Freezer paper

Stitch around motifs. This technique works best for machine quilting. Choose an interesting print for the back of your quilt, one that has medium to large flowers, leaves, plumes, animals, or something that relates nicely to your quilt top. Then machine quilt from the back of the quilt instead of the front. You can free-motion quilt around the motifs. Don't worry if you don't stay exactly on the lines. From the front of the quilt, the shapes will be recognizable, and you won't have any markings to remove.

Stitch through paper. Here's another option for machine quilters. Draw or photocopy designs onto paper that you can pin to your quilt top and stitch through. Tissue paper or other translucent paper works best because you can still see the quilt beneath the paper, and the paper will be easy to tear away when quilting is complete. You can even find ready-made motifs and border designs to stick on your quilt top for this type of quilting.

Marking Tools and Tips

When you do need to mark the quilting design on your quilt top, the method and tools that you choose should allow you to make a line dark enough to see while stitching, but also easy to remove. Before using any marking tool on your quilt top, make sure to test it on a scrap piece of fabric first.

Choose a Design

Determine what type of design you want to mark onto your quilt top. Large areas that commonly need quilting designs include plain alternate blocks, setting triangles, and borders. You can design your own motif, use a pattern from a book, or use a quilting stencil. Stencils are handy in that you can easily use a pencil to draw between the cutouts in the plastic to mark the design onto your fabric. They come in a huge array of designs, shapes, and sizes. This is the method that I am the most fond of. The drawback is that you can't resize stencils to fit different areas, so they are limited in where you can use them.

A paper pattern requires tracing, and possibly the use of a light box, but you can enlarge or reduce it on a photocopier to suit your needs. If you have a stencil that you want to use but the size is wrong, you can trace the design onto paper and enlarge or reduce it. You're no longer using it as a stencil, but you can still make use of the shape.

Stencils are available in a wide variety of motifs and sizes.

Choose a Marking Tool

Quilters have long debated the best tool for marking a quilt, and your choice may depend on whether you're marking dark or light fabrics and whether or not you plan to wash the finished quilt. Below, you'll find a list of the pros and cons of commonly available marking tools.

Mechanical pencil. Many quilters prefer to use a mechanical pencil. Because the lead breaks easily with too much pressure, it doesn't allow you to bear down too hard, thus avoiding an excessively dark line. In addition, the point always stays nice and sharp. Use a 0.5 mm lead in either medium (B) or medium hard (MB). If you wish to erase the lines when you are done quilting, there is an eraser made especially for cloth.

Colored pencils. When lead will not show up on certain colors, you will

have to choose another method. Some quilt shops carry colored marking pencils, such as yellow, pink, blue, and white. Choose and use these with caution. Often they are grease-based pencils, and the only way to remove the brightly colored markings is to use a grease-dissolving detergent.

Soap slivers or chalk markers. Both of these methods are good to use on dark fabrics. They make marks that are easy to see and easy to remove. The only drawback is that the edges dull very quickly. A chalk wheel is a related option. You don't have to worry about keeping a fine point, but the chalk brushes off quite easily, so it's best to mark as you go when using a chalk wheel.

Water-soluble marking pens. These pens are available in a variety of different colors. The ink contains a chemical that sometimes reacts unfavorably on certain fabrics, reappearing months later, sometimes in a brownish color. Using an iron over markings made by these pens can set the color, making them impossible to wash out. Use these markers with caution.

Air-erasable marking pens. Like the water-soluble pens, these pens feature disappearing ink—except this ink evaporates when exposed to the air, so you don't need to wash or wet your quilt to remove the ink. Take the same precautions—test first and don't iron the markings.

Also note that the markings only last about 24 to 48 hours, so don't mark an entire quilt top with one if you don't intend to complete the quilting in that amount of time. Markings tend to disappear faster in high humidity or when the quilt is exposed to direct light.

Hera. This plastic tool comes to us from Japan. It marks the fabric by creasing it rather than leaving a permanent mark. You don't have to worry about removing the markings, but it can be difficult to see the creases unless you have extremely good lighting.

A hera and ruler make quick work of marking cross-hatching patterns.

Mark the Quilt

The entire top may be marked before the three quilt layers are basted together, and if you're tracing a design, this is pretty much your only choice. Depending on what type of marker you use, however, some of the markings may wear off in the process of sandwiching the layers or before you are completely done with the quilting. Those areas can always be marked again.

If you're using a stencil to mark your quilt, you can do it either before layering and basting or afterward, marking as you go. The one drawback to marking as you go is that once the layers are basted, the quilt does have some loft, and it's a bit harder to use some markers accurately on the soft quilt. You can also consider a mix of the two, marking some intricate areas like feathered wreaths beforehand, and other less intricate parts block by block as you go.

To mark your quilt, lay it on a flat surface, with a stencil on top or the drawn pattern underneath. Trace around the design with your desired marking tool. If your fabric is too dark for you to see through to your pattern, you can use a light box, a light under a glass table, or even a window on a sunny day. The light showing through from the back of the fabric will enable you to see the design more clearly.

Layering and Basting the Quilt

Before you can start quilting, the quilt top, batting, and backing need to be made into a "sandwich" and basted together so that the layers don't shift. The basting method you use depends upon how you'll be quilting the project:
- If you plan to hand quilt in a hoop, you will need to baste the three layers together with thread.

If you're going to hand quilt on a frame, you may or may not need to baste the layers, depending on how your frame operates.

- If you plan to machine quilt at home, it's better to pin-baste with safety pins than to use thread. When you sew over basting threads it is hard to remove them later. Safety pins, on the other hand, can be removed one at a time as you approach them.

- If you plan to send your quilt to a professional quilter, either a long-arm machine quilter or a hand quilter, you do not need to baste the layers together. Long-arm machine quilters attach the backing and batting fabric on separate canvas leaders on the machine's rollers, and the batting is then rolled between the layers as the quilting progresses. Hand quilters may baste the quilt for you on their frame, allowing you to skip this task.

Preparation

It helps to have a large table that is the proper height, since this job can be rather time-consuming and rough on the back, especially if you're working on a large quilt. Most people do not have this luxury at home, so a floor is usually the only place large enough to do it. Carpeting is a help but not absolutely necessary. Sometimes public buildings such as libraries or churches will permit you to use a community room with tables that can be pushed together for an afternoon of basting, so ask around. You may be able to avoid crawling around on your knees.

1. Press the quilt back. Spread it out, smoothing all wrinkles. If you're basting on a table, try fastening the edges to the table with large binder clips. If you're basting on the floor, tape the backing in place. If your floor is carpeted, you can pin the edges of the quilt into the carpet with large T pins. The object is to make the sure that the backing stays smooth, flat, and wrinkle free, but to not stretch it out of shape.

2. Center the batting over the backing, smoothing out all wrinkles and working any fullness toward the edges with your hands. Make sure the batting is flat, but do not stretch it. Trim the excess so that the batting is even with the backing. If your batting has stubborn creases from being folded in a package, you can let it lie flat for 24 hours or try fluffing it in a dryer on the lowest setting for about 15 minutes. The air will help relax the wrinkles.

3. Check the wrong side of the quilt top for any errant threads that need to be clipped and for seams that may be twisted. If necessary, re-press. Then place the quilt top on top of the bat-

ting, aligning the center of the quilt with the center of the backing. Smooth out all wrinkles with your hands by working from the center to the outer edges, again taking care not to stretch any part of the quilt out of shape.

Pin Basting

If you are machine quilting at home on your sewing machine, pin the layers together with 1"-long safety pins. Begin pinning at the center of the quilt, working your way to the outer edges. Place pins about 3" to 4" apart. Check to make sure that the layers aren't shifting. If necessary, add more pins at closer intervals to keep the layers securely in place. When sewing, remove each pin before you come to it.

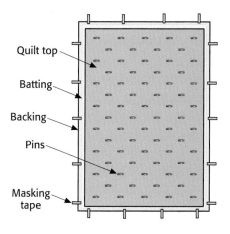

Thread Basting for Hand Quilting

Using light-colored thread and a long needle, start in the center of the quilt and take long running stitches toward one corner of the quilt. Repeat, basting to each corner to make an X through the quilt. Continue basting the remainder of the quilt in a grid pattern, making the stitching lines about 6" to 8" apart. To finish, baste along all outside edges.

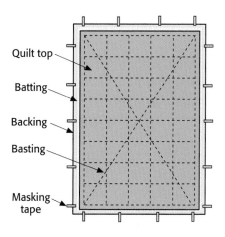

Machine Quilting

These days, more and more quiltmakers are using their home sewing machines to quilt their projects because it's faster than hand quilting and makes for a durable finished quilt. Entire books have been written on the subject about the fine points of machine quilting. Here we'll touch on some of the basics and on areas that are likely problem-causers so that you can hopefully avoid them on your next project.

Needles, Threads, and Tension

When it comes to machine quilting, you have a lot of thread options: cotton, rayon, metallic, monofilament, and a whole lot more. The key thing to remember about thread is that you need to use an appropriate needle to match the style of your thread. Machine needles all have a groove on one side and a scarf (a shorter groove) on the other side. These features give the thread a place to glide along the needle as the needle goes in and out of the fabric. The groove and the scarf size vary, depending on the style of needle.

For machine quilting, you can choose quilting needles, which have a deeper scarf so that the thread can easily travel through more layers than in patchwork. These needles work fine for cotton quilting thread. For other threads, you may be better off with another type of needle. If you're stitching with metallic threads or Mylar, use a metallic needle. If you're using rayon or some other type of decorative thread, you might want to try an embroidery needle, which is designed specifically for use with these threads.

In addition to a needle with a deeper scarf, you'll want to use a needle that's a larger size than you'd use for patchwork. While a 75/11 or 80/12 works great for sewing through patchwork seams, a 90/14 will make a bigger hole, allowing the heavier quilting thread to travel smoothly down through the quilt top, batting, and backing—and back up again.

In your bobbin, you can use quilting thread to match the top thread, or use a thread to match the backing. Just be sure to test your thread combination on a sample quilt sandwich to make sure the tension is adjusted properly. If the bobbin thread is pulling up to the top, loosen the top thread tension. If too much top thread is pulling to the back of the quilt, tighten the top thread tension.

Using a Walking Foot

Most quilters start their foray into machine quilting by using a walking foot or even-feed foot. This device helps feed the top of the quilt through the machine at the same pace that the feed dogs pull the bottom layer through the machine, helping you form nice, even stitches without shifting the quilt layers as you sew. You can use a walking foot for stitching straight lines (quilting in the ditch and crosshatching) and gentle curves.

Walking Foot

1. Put the needle in the fabric and turn the handwheel to pull up the needle and thus the bobbin thread. Set the stitch length to zero and take two or three stitches in the same place to lock the thread.

2. Set the stitch length to slightly longer than you'd use for patchwork. Because of the depth of the multiple layers, a little extra length on your stitches will look nicely spaced. Begin stitching, following your marked pattern or stitching in the ditch.

⮕ TAKE THE ⬅
LOW ROAD

When stitching in the ditch, it's easiest to sew on the low side of the seam—the side opposite the side to which the seam allowances have been pressed. This way, you're stitching through three layers rather than five (the three quilt layers plus the two seam allowances). It's easier to stitch, and you'll be less likely to stitch a pucker into the layers.

---

3. Continue sewing to the opposite side of the quilt or to wherever your straight line ends. If feasible, turn the corner and keep sewing without breaking the thread. If you need to stop and restart elsewhere, set the stitch length to zero, take two or three stitches to anchor the thread, and then lift the needle from the fabric. Do not cut the thread.

4. Move the quilt to the next starting place, lower the needle, and begin again by taking a few anchoring stitches. After you begin stitching, you can clip the thread that connects your stopping and new starting points. This kind of connect-the-dots maneuvering saves you thread and the time it takes to repeatedly take your quilt out of the machine to clip threads. When all quilting is completed, you can snip all the threads at once from the back of the quilt.

Free-Motion Quilting

Once you're confident with straight-line quilting, you'll probably be ready to add more variety to your repertoire. To easily stitch more intricate shapes, such as feathers, stippling, meandering, and more, you'll need to do free-motion quilting. With this method, you move the quilt in the direction you want rather than have the machine move it in a straight line for you. It takes a bit of practice to coordinate your hand motions with the speed of the machine, but mastering free-motion quilting is liberating.

To do free-motion machine quilting, you will need to lower the feed dogs on your machine (or cover them with a business card if they can't be lowered) and use a darning foot. Many machines come with a darning foot, or you can purchase one as a special attachment. A darning foot is round (or oval), sometimes a complete circle, and sometimes with an opening for better visibility. A darning foot hops up and down as the machine sews, enabling you to move the fabric beneath it as the stitches are formed. The length of the stitch is controlled by the speed at which you move the fabric.

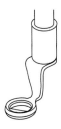

Darning Foot

1. Set the stitch length to zero, and start and stop stitching as described in "Using a Walking Foot" on page 116.
2. To move the fabric to follow the design, it's easiest to focus on one 12" x 12" area at a time. The rest of the quilt can be rolled up to fit under the arm of the machine; only the area that you're focusing on needs to be smooth and flat.

⁓ SET UP ⁓ FOR SUCCESS

When machine quilting, you may need to rearrange your sewing space a bit to make it more comfortable and conducive to quilting rather than sewing. It is handy to have a large work surface by your sewing machine to support the quilt layers as you manipulate them through the machine.

If you do not have a large sewing table, you can extend yours by placing a card table or other side table to the left or back of your machine to hold up the parts of the quilt you aren't working on. Otherwise you will have to roll the quilt and secure it, leaving flat only the small area that you are working on. If you let the quilt droop over the side of your sewing table, it will cause a lot of drag as you sew, possibly distorting your stitches and causing you to fatigue sooner.

Hand Quilting

Hand quilting is a time-honored method for finishing patchwork and appliqué quilts. Hand quilting is a series of small running stitches that travel through the three quilt layers to hold them together. Many quilters pride themselves on their small, even stitches, but if you're new to hand quilting, strive for *even-length* stitches. As you become more experienced, smaller stitches will follow.

Supplies for Hand Quilting

For this part of the quilting process, you need relatively few tools or notions. The basics are a thimble to protect your sewing finger, quilting thread, needles, a pair of scissors, and something to hold your quilt taut as you sew.

Needles and thread. Use Betweens, which are short, sturdy needles made expressly for this job. The larger the number on the package, the smaller the needle—and the smaller the eye, so threading can be challenging. Use thread made for hand quilting. It is often glazed or coated, giving it a sturdier finish than regular sewing thread.

Thimble. Thimbles are available in so many styles. Metal, leather, plastic, closed top, open top for your fingernail, thumb thimbles, and so on. You will need a thimble for your middle finger of the hand that holds the needle, to protect it as you push the needle through the thickness of the quilt. Try a variety of thimbles to see which works best for you.

Hoop. A quilting hoop lets you hold the layers of your quilt taut so that they don't shift during quilting. Using a hoop makes your quilting portable, since you can carry it with you. When you place your quilt in a hoop, don't pull the layers so tightly that you can bounce a coin on the fabric. You need to have a little bit of give for working the needle in and out of the layers. Hoops are available in handheld, lap, and floor models. Their size and shape also vary, from 12" to 18" or larger, in round models as well as oval and even square models.

Quilting frame. As an alternative to a hoop, a frame will accommodate the entire quilt; the portions of the quilt not being worked on are typically rolled up on bars. When you finish quilting a portion of the quilt, you release the bars, roll up the finished section, and position the next section in the middle of the frame for quilting. Frames are typically made of wood and can be as simple as two-by-fours clamped onto sawhorses or as complex as ones with separate ratchet systems that allow you to roll each layer separately, thus eliminating the need for basting. You can also find less expensive models made of PVC piping that have snap-on cuffs that hold the quilt to the frame.

A basic model quilt frame uses C-clamps to hold the bars to the legs.

PVC frames come in a variety of square and rectangular sizes and can be attached to legs to make them free standing.

⋙ SORE FINGER ⋙

Hand quilting requires that you hold your nonsewing hand beneath the quilt to feel when the needle has made its way through all the layers. The finger that is used to feel the needle is invariably going to become sore from being pricked. I am fortunate that I am a cellist and have very heavily callused left fingertips. However, there are many special thimbles and finger coverings that are available to help protect your fingertips. Some are soft sided, some stick on with adhesive, and some look like thimbles with cutaway portions. The only way to find out what works best is to experiment.

The Quilting Process

Choose a Between needle in a size that's comfortable for you. These needles come in sizes from 1 to 12, although most shops don't carry Between needles larger than size 7. Remember, for hand-sewing needles, the higher the number, the smaller the needle. The smaller the needle, the smaller your stitches will be. For beginners, I recommend starting with a size 8 or 9 needle, since it will be easy for you to maneuver. As you grow accustomed to the process, you may want to switch to smaller needles, such as a size 10 or even a size 12.

1. Use a single strand of thread about 18" long; make a knot at the end.

2. Bury the knot by placing the needle through the quilt top about 1" or so from where you wish to begin quilting. Tunnel through the batting and come up through the quilt top where you want to make the first stitch. Gently pull the thread until the knot pops through the quilt top and becomes secured in the batting.

3. Make one small backstitch, and then continue quilting with running stitches. Use the thimble to push the needle through the quilt, and place your other hand under the quilt so that you can feel when the needle comes through the backing. When you feel the tip of the needle underneath the quilt, use your thimble finger to rock the needle back up through the layers. By feeling each prick underneath the quilt, you'll be sure the needle has penetrated the layers. You can rock the needle back and forth, packing a few stitches onto the

shank of the needle. Then pull the needle out of the quilt top and gently tug the thread so that it is taut. Don't pull too tightly or the thread will gather the quilt layers. Continue stitching in this manner until you are almost out of thread.

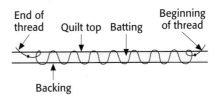

4. Bury the knot at the end. Make a small knot in your thread, about ½" from the last stitch. Make a small backstitch, running the thread through the batting and coming up again about ½" away from the stitching. Pull gently until the knot snaps through the quilt top and embeds in the batting. Clip the thread close to the quilt top.

～ PRACTICE ～
EVEN STITCHING

Like anything else, hand quilting takes practice before your stitches become even and tiny. Strive for stitches that are the same length as the spaces between them. If the spacing is consistent, your quilting will look nicer than if you have some very tiny stitches sprinkled in with larger ones. As you become more comfortable with making even stitches, you'll be ready to use smaller needles, which are the key to smaller stitches.

Seven to nine stitches per inch is considered very good quilting. Nine to twelve is excellent, and anything higher is stupendous. Your quilting should look as good from the front as it does from the back.

Tying a Quilt

Quilts that are tied rather than quilted are generally called comforters. They are apt to have a higher loft batting. You'll need to baste your quilt top for tying, just as you would for quilting. You can use worsted-weight yarn, pearl cotton, or six-strand embroidery floss for ties. Your ties should be spaced no more than 4" apart to ensure that the layers will not shift during use.

1. Thread a long needle with an 18" length of yarn, floss, or pearl cotton.
2. Take a stitch through all layers, coming up again close to where you went through. Cut the yarn to about 4" long.

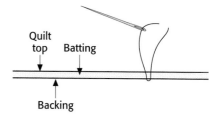

3. Make a square knot by wrapping the right tail around the left tail and tighten; wrap the left tail around the right tail and tighten again.
4. Trim ends even, about ½" long.

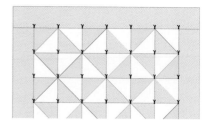

CHAPTER 12

BINDING AND FINISHING TOUCHES

ONCE THE QUILTING IS COMPLETE, IT IS TIME TO CLEAN UP THE EDGES AND APPLY BINDING TO COVER THE RAW EDGES AND BATTING. IN THIS CHAPTER WE'LL REVIEW MAKING STRAIGHT-GRAIN AND BIAS BINDING, MITERING CORNERS, FINISHING THE ENDS OF BINDING, ADDING A HANGING SLEEVE, AND LABELING YOUR QUILT.

Binding Preparation

Before attaching binding to your quilt, you'll need to trim off the excess batting and backing fabric and make sure the quilt top is square. Also remove any basting threads or pins that weren't removed during the quilting process.

1. Using a rotary cutter and long ruler, trim the batting and backing so that they are even with the edges of the quilt top.

2. Check the corners of the quilt to make sure they are square. (A larger square ruler is good for this purpose.) Trim the corners, if necessary, to square them.

Straight-Grain versus Bias Binding

Straight-grain binding is fine for most quilts. Bias binding is used for quilts with curved edges and, because it tends to wear longer, for quilts that will get heavy use. You might also want to consider bias binding if you are using a fabric that would look more interesting if it were cut on the bias, such as a plaid or stripe. The difference in making the two types of binding is merely in how you cut the strips. After that, they are sewn together and attached to the quilt in the same manner.

Cutting Straight-Grain Strips

You can cut binding strips from the crosswise or lengthwise grain of the fabric. Crosswise strips are more common because they're easier to cut, and even with lengthwise strips you'll need to seam strips together to make a continuous binding. Strips are generally cut 2" to 2½" wide, depending on your preference for binding width.

Cut enough strips to go around the perimeter of your quilt plus about 10" extra for mitering the corners and joining the strips at the end. To determine how much binding fabric you'll need, see the chart on page 137.

1. Overlap the strips, right sides together, at a 90° angle. Sew the strips together, stitching from one intersection point to the other.
2. Trim the excess fabric, leaving a ¼" seam allowance. Press the seam allowance open.

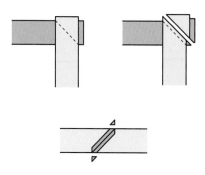

3. Fold the strips in half lengthwise, with wrong sides together. Press.

Cutting Bias Binding

1. Straighten one edge of the fabric with your rotary cutter and ruler. (See page 24.)
2. Fold one corner of the fabric diagonally so that the cut edge aligns with the adjacent selvage.
3. Align your long rotary-cutting ruler so that the 45° marking line is parallel with the selvage, and the long edge of the ruler is just inside the folded diagonal edge as shown. Trim off the fold.

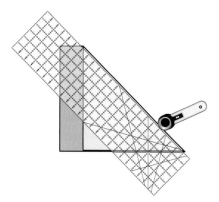

4. Remove the large triangle of fabric and set aside. Align your ruler along the diagonally cut edge to cut binding strips to your desired width.
5. Sew the strips together, end to end, and press the seams open. Fold the long strip in half lengthwise, wrong sides together, and press.

Attaching Binding

Binding can be attached to the quilt with mitered corners, butted corners, or even to rounded corners. Each method is explained below.

Mitered Corners

1. Begin stitching the binding to the quilt along one side, not at a corner. Match the raw edge of the binding with the raw edge of the quilt. Leaving about a 5" tail of binding, start sewing, using a ¼" seam allowance.

2. Stop sewing ¼" from the corner; backstitch and remove the quilt from the machine.

3. Turn the quilt so that you will be ready to sew the next edge. First, fold the binding so that it is straight up in line with the edge you will now be sewing. Then fold it down and align it with the edge that you will be sewing. Align the fold with the corner of the quilt top.

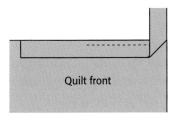

Quilt front

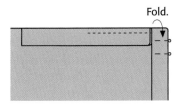

Fold.

4. Sew along the second edge in the same fashion, stopping ¼" from the corner. Fold the next miter and continue, stitching each side and mitering the corners as you go.

5. Stop stitching about 7" away from the point where you started attaching the binding, and backstitch. Remove the quilt from the machine.

6. Overlap the beginning and ending tails of the binding. Mark the overlap by the same distance as your binding strips are wide. For instance, if you are using 2"-wide binding, mark a 2" overlap. If you're using 2½"-wide strips, the overlap should be 2½". Trim each end of the binding at the marked points.

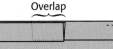

Overlap

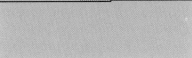

7. Open the folds of the two ends of the binding and overlap the ends at right angles, right sides together as shown. Pin the ends

together and draw the seam line diagonally between the points where the strips intersect.

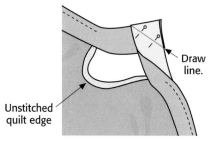

Draw line.

Unstitched quilt edge

8. Sew the binding ends together along the drawn line. Trim the excess fabric, leaving a ¼" seam allowance. Finger-press the seam open. Then refold the binding and sew it in place on the quilt.

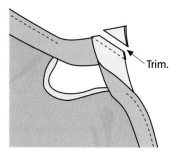

Trim.

9. Fold the binding to the back of the quilt so that it covers the machine stitching. Pin in place. Blind stitch in place (see page 56 for the appliqué stitch), folding the miters in place as you reach each corner. Stitch the miters in place on both the back and front of the quilt.

⌒ BINDING SEAMS ⌒ AT QUILT CORNERS

With a continuous binding, there is a possibility that you may encounter a seam in the binding that will fall at the corner of the quilt where you plan to miter. If this should happen, you have two options. First, you can proceed as normal, ignoring the seam. There will be slightly more bulk at the corner but no extra steps to finish the binding. The other option is to stop stitching, remove the quilt from the machine, and cut out the offending binding seam. Trim the end of the attached binding, and then resew it to the other section of the binding. This way the binding seam will fall a few inches before the corner of the quilt, enabling you to make a smooth miter.

Overlapped Corners

In this method, the binding is applied separately to each side of the quilt. This is typically how Amish quilts are bound. Cut (or piece) a binding strip to fit each of the four sides of the quilt, making each one about 4" longer than the quilt measurement.

1. Fold each binding strip in half lengthwise with wrong sides together and press. Aligning the raw edges, stitch the top and bottom binding strips to the top and bottom of the quilt.

2. Fold the binding strips to the back of the quilt and slipstitch them in place. Trim the binding edges flush with the quilt.

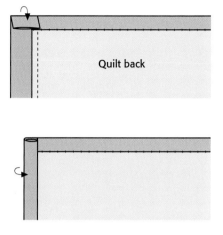

Quilt back

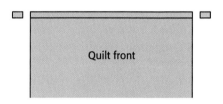

Quilt front

3. Sew the side bindings to the quilt in the same manner, leaving about 2" extending on each end. Trim away the excess binding, leaving a ¼" extension on each end for turning under.

4. Fold the cut ends of the bindings over the binding strips that are already stitched in place. Then fold the binding to the back of the quilt and slipstitch in place. Stitch the corners so that they are secure.

Rounded Corners

Some quilts look nice with rounded corners. If you want to round off the corners of your quilt, use a circle template or something that's even handier—a dinner plate—to mark the curve. Trim away the excess fabric and you have rounded corners. To bind them, you'll need to use bias binding. Apply the binding as for "Mitered Corners" on page 125. Of course, you won't have corners to miter, but the rest of the steps for attaching and finishing the binding are the same.

Be sure to gently ease the binding around the corners, taking care not to stretch it as you sew around the curves. Otherwise, the corners will not lie flat.

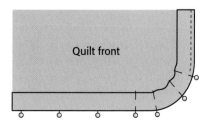

Quilt front

Quick Machine Binding

If you wish to avoid hand sewing the binding, and you don't mind if an extra row of stitching shows on the back of the quilt, try this quick machine method for binding.

1. After squaring up the quilt, sew the binding to the back of the quilt rather than to the quilt top, using a ¼" seam allowance and mitering the corners as usual.

2. Turn the binding to the front of the quilt and carefully pin the binding all around the perimeter, making sure to securely pin the corners. Be sure that the binding covers the machine stitching.

3. Sewing slowly, machine stitch the folded edge of the binding to the right side of the quilt. It is hard to control where the stitching is going on the back of the quilt, but aim for a nice straight line along the folded edge of the binding on the top of the quilt. Do not sew through the mitered part of the corners, but go back afterward and secure these with hand stitching.

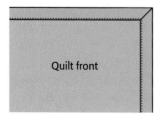

Quilt front

Signing Your Quilt

Some quilters like to sign their name and date to the finished quilt. You can use a permanent marker to do this in a corner of the quilt, or you can make or buy a quilt label. I like to buy the pretty labels that are printed on fabric. I write in the information with a permanent marker, then slipstitch the label to the lower corner of the quilt. I have also embroidered my initials and the date on the quilt front or back.

Adding a label is especially nice if the quilt is for a gift or special occasion. You can add all pertinent information about the recipient, about you, and when you made the quilt. However, it's also a good idea to sign and date quilts that aren't intended as gifts. This way, future generations will have information about who made the quilt, and it won't become a mystery as so many antique quilts are to us today.

Hanging Your Quilt

There are several ways to display a quilt, the most obvious one being on a bed! Wooden quilt racks are a beautiful option; draped over a staircase railing is another. You can also find quilt hangers that clamp over the top of the quilt, allowing it to be hung from a wall.

If you wish to hang the quilt from the wall by threading a dowel or curtain rod through it, you will need to sew a sleeve to the back of the quilt. The main point to consider is that the quilt's weight must be evenly distributed. If not, certain points will bear the stress, and a damaged and misshapen quilt will be the result. If you want to hang a bed-size quilt on the wall, it's a good idea to make a split sleeve—two smaller sleeves with a break in the center of the quilt—so that a support bracket or nail can be used at the center in addition to at the two ends.

Hanging Sleeve Before Binding

To attach a hanging sleeve *before* the binding is applied:

1. Cut a piece of fabric the width of the quilt by 8½". This will yield a 4"-wide finished sleeve.
2. To hem the short ends of the sleeve, fold under ¼" at each end, and then fold under ¼" again. Stitch the folds in place.
3. Fold the sleeve in half lengthwise with wrong sides together. Press.
4. Place the raw edges of the sleeve flush with the unbound quilt top. When you sew the binding in place, you will be attaching the top of the sleeve at the same time. The raw edges will be covered by the binding when it is folded to the back of the quilt.

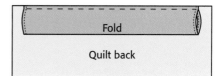

5. Hand sew the bottom of the sleeve to the back of the quilt, being careful to not have your stitches go through to the front of the quilt.

Hanging Sleeve After Binding

To attach a hanging sleeve *after* the binding is applied:

1. Make the sleeve as described in steps 1 and 2, at left.
2. With wrong sides together, sew the raw edges together, and then press the seam allowance open.
3. Position the sleeve so that the seam is centered along the underside.
4. Pin the sleeve to the back of the quilt, just below the bound edge. Whipstitch both the top and the bottom of the sleeve to the quilt, being careful that your stitches don't go through to the front of the quilt.

CHAPTER 13

HANDY CHARTS AND MATH CHEAT SHEETS

EVEN IF ALGEBRA AND GEOMETRY WEREN'T YOUR FAVORITE HIGH SCHOOL SUBJECTS, IT'S GOOD TO KNOW A FEW BASIC EQUATIONS WHEN IT COMES TO QUILTING. THAT WAY YOU CAN CALCULATE SIZES FOR SETTING TRIANGLES, TRIANGLE SQUARES, AND SUCH TO FIT PRECISELY IN YOUR QUILT PLAN.

You'll find lots of charts in this chapter so that you can easily look up what you need to know. But first, let's look at the common formulas used so you can "do the math" whenever you need to.

Diagonal measurement of a square: 1.414 x length of one side

Half-square triangles: Cut square the desired finished size plus ⅞" for seam allowances. Cut once diagonally to yield two triangles.

Quarter-square triangles: Cut square the desired finished length of the base of the triangle plus 1¼". Cut twice diagonally to yield four quarter-square triangles.

Side setting triangles: Multiply the finished block by 1.414; add 1¼" for seam allowances, and round up to the nearest ⅛" increment. Cut squares this size and cut them twice diagonally to yield four setting triangles.

Corner setting triangles: Divide the finished block size by 1.414; add ⅞" for seam allowances, and round up to the nearest ⅛" increment. Cut squares this size and cut them once diagonally to yield two corner triangles.

Side setting triangles with sashing: Add two times the finished width of the sashing to the finished block size; multiply the result by 1.414; add 1¼" for seam allowances. Cut squares this size and cut them twice diagonally to yield four setting triangles.

Corner setting triangles with sashing: Add two times the finished width of the sashing to the finished block size; divide the result by 1.414; add ⅞" for seam allowances. Cut squares this size and then cut once diagonally to yield two corner triangles.

Needle Sizes: European/American

For lightweight fabrics, use sizes 60/8 to 75/11; for mid-weight fabrics, use sizes 80/12 to 90/14; for heavyweight fabrics, use sizes 100/16 to 120/20.

European	60	65	70	75	80	90	100	110	120
U.S.	8	9	10	11	12	14	16	18	20

Stitch Length

On most machines, the numbers for stitch length refer to millimeters.

Millimeters	Stitches per Inch
.5	50
1	25
1.5	16
2	12
2.5	10
3	8
3.5	7
4	6
4.5–5	5

Decimals to Fractions

Decimal	Fraction
.125	1/8
.1875	3/16
.25	1/4
.3333	1/3
.375	3/8
.5	1/2
.625	5/8
.6666	2/3
.75	3/4
.875	7/8

Block Size x Blocks per Row = Quilt Size

Block size and blocks per row determine the size of your quilt. To find the width of your quilt, first locate the size of your blocks in the left column. Then read across the top of the chart and stop at the number that corresponds with the blocks in your *horizontal* row. Draw imaginary lines from each point until they intersect; the measurement at their intersection point is the width of your quilt. To find the length of your quilt, again locate your block size in the left column. At the top of chart, select the number that corresponds with the blocks in your *vertical* row. The point where these two columns intersect is your quilt width. Note that these measurements do not include borders.

Block Size	Blocks per Row									
	4	5	6	7	8	9	10	11	12	13
6"	24"	30"	36"	42"	48"	54"	60"	66"	72"	78"
6½"	26"	32½"	39"	45½"	52"	58½"	65"	71½"	78"	84½"
7"	28"	35"	42"	49"	56"	63"	70"	77"	84"	91"
7½"	30"	37½"	45"	52½"	60"	67½"	75"	82½"	90"	97½"
8"	32"	40"	48"	56"	64"	72"	80"	88"	96"	104"
8½"	34"	42½"	51"	59½"	68"	76½"	85"	93½"	102"	110½"
9"	36"	45"	54"	63"	72"	81"	90"	99"	108"	117"
9½"	38"	47½"	57"	66½"	76"	85½"	95"	104½"	114"	
10"	40"	50"	60"	70"	80"	90"	100"	110"	120"	
10½"	42"	52½"	63"	73½"	84"	94½"	105"	115½"		
11"	44"	55"	66"	77"	88"	99"	110"	121"		
11½"	46"	57½"	69"	80½"	92"	103½"	115"			
12"	48"	60"	72"	84"	96"	108"	120"			
12½"	50"	62½"	75"	87½"	100"	112½"				
13"	52"	65"	78"	91"	104"	117"				
13½"	54"	67½"	81"	94½"	108"	121½"				
14"	56"	70"	84"	98"	112"					
14½"	58"	72½"	87"	101½"	116"					
15"	60"	75"	90"	105"	120"					
15½"	62"	77½"	93"	108½"						
16"	64"	80"	96"	112"						

Diagonal Measurement of Squares

The diagonal measurement of a square is 1.414 times the length of the square. The diagonal measurement of your quilt block is used to calculate sizes for side setting triangles and corner setting triangles as well as the overall size of an on-point quilt. The calculations given here have been rounded up to the nearest ⅛" and seam allowances have been added. If you prefer to cut setting triangles oversized, you'll need to start with a larger square.

Block Size	Diagonal	Size to Cut Squares for Side Setting Triangles	Size to Cut Squares for Corner Setting Triangles
1½"	2.12	3⅜"	2"
2"	2.83	4⅛"	2⅜"
3"	4.24	5½"	3"
4"	5.65	7"	3¾"
5"	7.07	8⅜"	4½"
6"	8.48	9¾"	5⅛"
7"	9.90	11⅛"	5⅞"
8"	11.31	12⅝"	6⅝"
9"	12.73	14"	7¾"
10"	14.14	15½"	8"
11"	15.6	16⅞"	8¾"
12"	16.97	18¼"	9⅜"
13"	18.38	19¾"	10⅛"
14"	19.80	21⅛"	10⅞"
15"	21.21	22½"	11½"
16"	22.62	23⅞"	12¼"
17"	24.04	25⅜"	13"
18"	25.45	26¾"	13⅝"
19"	26.87	28⅛"	14⅜"
20"	28.28	29⅝"	15⅛"

Blocks Needed for Diagonal Settings

Blocks Across by Blocks Down	Number of Blocks	Number of Side Triangles
4 x 6	39	16
5 x 5	41	16
6 x 6	61	20
6 x 8	83	24
7 x 7	85	24
8 x 9	138	30
10 x 10	181	36
10 x 12	219	40
4 corner triangles are required for all sizes.		

Blocks Needed for Two-Block Settings

Blocks Across by Blocks Down	Design Blocks	Alternate Blocks	Total Blocks
3 x 5	7	8	15
5 x 7	18	17	35
7 x 9	32	31	63
9 x 11	50	49	99

Yardage Equivalents

Yardage Amount	Inches	Decimal
⅛ yard	4½"	.125
¼ yard	9"	.25
⅓ yard	12"	.333
⅜ yard	13½"	.375
½ yard	18"	.50
⅝ yard	22½"	.625
⅔ yard	24"	.666
¾ yard	27"	.75
⅞ yard	31½"	.875
1 yard	36"	1.00

Standard Mattress Dimensions in Inches (Surface Only)

Mattress thicknesses vary. If you want your quilt to have a particular drop, measure the distance from the top of the mattress to that point.

Bassinet	13" x 28"
Crib	23" x 46"
Playpen	40" x 40"
Youth	32" x 66"
Studio	30" x 75"
Bunk	38" x 75"
Twin	39" x 75"
Long Twin	39" x 89"
Double	54" x 75"
Queen	60" x 80"
King	78" x 80"
California King	72" x 84"

Comforter Sizes

Commercial comforters are generally a standard size and are designed to be used as a bed topper. They do not necessarily cover the box spring and do not have a pillow tuck. Their standard sizes are as follows:

Twin	65" x 88"
Full	80" x 88"
Queen	86" x 93"
King	104" x 93"

Bedspread Sizes

Commercial bedspreads cover the bed and fall almost to the floor. They also have a pillow tuck. Below are the measurements based on a 21" drop and an 11" pillow tuck. Note that if you have a pillow-top mattress, you may need a longer drop to cover the sides of the mattress and boxspring.

Twin	81" x 107"
Full	96" x 107"
Queen	102" x 112"
King	120" x 112"

Number of Squares Yielded from 42"-Wide Fabric

Finished Size	¼ yard	½ yard	¾ yard	1 yard
1"	168	336	504	672
1½"	84	189	273	378
2"	48	112	160	224
2½"	42	84	126	168
3"	24	60	84	120
3½"	20	40	60	90
4"	18	36	54	72
4½"	8	24	40	56
5"	7	21	28	42
5½"	7	21	28	42
6"	6	12	24	30

Number of Half-Square Triangles Yielded from 42"-Wide Fabric

Finished Size	¼ yard	½ yard	¾ yard	1 yard
1"	168	378	546	756
1½"	96	224	320	448
2"	84	168	252	336
2½"	48	120	168	240
3"	40	80	120	180
3½"	36	72	108	144
4"	16	48	80	112
4½"	14	42	56	84
5"	14	42	56	84

Yardage Needed for ½"-Wide (Finished) Straight-Grain Binding

Quilt Size	Number of 2½"- Wide Strips	Inches of Fabric	Yards of Fabric
36" x 36"	4	12½"	3/8
54" x 90"	8	20"	5/8
72" x 90"	8	20"	5/8
90" x 108"	10	25"	3/4
120" x 120"	12	30"	7/8

Yardage Needed for ½"-Wide (Finished) Bias Binding

Quilt Size	Yards of Bias Needed	Yards of Fabric
36" x 36"	4½	½ yard
54" x 90"	8½	5/8 yard
72" x 90"	9½	5/8 yard
90" x 108"	11½	3/4 yard
120" x 120"	14½	1 yard

Yardage Needed for ½"-Wide (Finished) Bias Binding

Yardage	Yields Inches of Bias
¼ yard	115"
3/8 yard	180"
½ yard	255"
5/8 yard	320"
3/4 yard	400"
7/8 yard	465"

Alternate blocks. Plain blocks that are usually set alternately with patterned blocks (either patchwork or appliqué).

Appliqué. The art of sewing small pieces of fabric onto a background fabric to create a design. Also the fabric pieces that form the design.

Backing. The large piece of fabric (or sewn-together pieces of fabric) that is layered beneath the quilt top and batting to make up the back of the quilt.

Bar sets. Vertical rows of quilt blocks separated by long strips (pieced or plain) of fabric.

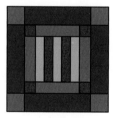

Amish Bars

Batting. The fiber used between the quilt top and quilt backing to give the quilt depth and warmth. Batting may be made of cotton, polyester, wool, or a blend of these fibers.

Bias. A diagonal line that runs at a 45° angle to the lengthwise and crosswise grain. Fabric cut on the bias has the most stretch.

Bias binding. Quilt binding made by cutting strips on the bias. Bias binding is generally more durable than binding cut on the straight grain of fabric.

Block. A quilt unit; can be pieced, appliquéd, or plain fabric. Most are square, but blocks can also be rectangular, hexagonal, and diamond shaped.

Border. The outside strips of fabric that frame the quilt blocks.

Butted corners. The corners made by sewing a border or binding onto the horizontal and vertical sides of a quilt without mitering.

Color wheel. A circular arrangement of colors showing the relationships between primary, secondary, and tertiary colors, and color schemes involving two or more colors.

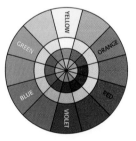

Cornerstones. Squares at the junctions of the vertical and horizontal border or sashing pieces; also called "sashing squares."

Crocking. The bleeding of excess dye from fabric when it is washed.

Crosswise grain. The threads of a fabric that run perpendicular to the selvage.

Design wall. A piece of quilt batting, felt, or other surface hung on a wall that allows the quilt designer to place fabric patches in designs to simulate the finished look of a quilt block or quilt layout.

Diagonal set. A quilt setting in which the blocks are arranged at a 45° angle to the sides of the quilt. This type of setting is also known as an on-point set.

Drafting. The art of drawing a quilt design to make templates or determine what size to cut each shape.

Fat quarter. A ½ yard length of fabric that is cut in half along the lengthwise fold to yield approximately 18" x 21" of fabric. This cut offers the same number of square inches as a traditional quarter yard of fabric, which measures 9" x 42", but results in a wider, more usable piece of fabric.

Feed dogs. The mechanism on a sewing machine that gently pushes the fabric under the presser foot.

Four Patch. A traditional block composed of four squares.

Grain of fabric. The lengthwise and crosswise threads of a fabric.

Intensity. The brightness or dullness of a color.

Lengthwise grain. The threads of a fabric that run parallel to the selvage.

Lightfast. Color that is resistant to fading when exposed to light.

Linking blocks. Alternate blocks that make a secondary pattern when combined with the primary blocks of the quilt.

Loft. The thickness of batting.

Medallion set. A quilt setting that features a central motif surrounded by setting triangles, quilt blocks, or borders.

Mitered corners. Corners that are joined at a 45° angle.

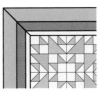

Presser foot. A sewing machine attachment that holds the fabric in place while sewing. Presser feet are available in different styles for different functions.

Prewashing. Washing fabric to remove excess dye and to preshrink it before it is used for quilting.

Quarter-square units. A pieced square composed of four triangles in an hourglass formation.

Rotary cutter. A cutting device with a handle and circular blade that allows several thicknesses of fabric to be cut at one time.

Sashing. Vertical and horizontal bars of fabric stitched between quilt blocks to separate them. Sashing can be single pieces of fabric or pieced units.

Seam allowance. The width of a seam. The standard seam allowance in quiltmaking is ¼".

Set or setting. The way in which the quilt blocks are put together, such as in horizontal and vertical rows, diagonal rows, or in vertical rows separated by lengthwise sashing strips.

Set-in seams. A place where three different patches intersect in the shape of a Y. Each part of the three-seam junction is stitched separately, leaving the seam allowance free in order to fit in each piece without puckers.

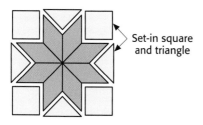

Set-in square and triangle

Setting triangles. The filler triangle pieces that are needed in a diagonal set to make the sides of the quilt straight rather than zigzagged.

Sewing-machine tension. The relationship between the top thread and bobbin thread that allows for a smooth, even stitch to be produced.

Shrinkage. The loss of fabric surface area due to washing, drying, or quilting.

Sleeve. A tube of fabric sewn to the back of the quilt that allows a rod to be inserted for hanging purposes.

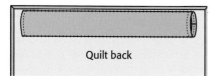

Quilt back

Straight set. A quilt setting in which the blocks are arranged in horizontal and vertical rows.

Straight-grain binding. Quilt binding made by cutting strips from the crosswise or lengthwise grain of the fabric. This type of binding requires less fabric than bias binding but isn't quite as durable.

Strip piecing. A technique of sewing strips of fabric together, and then cutting them into certain shapes or units.

Template. A shape made from a firm material and used as a guide for marking fabric for cutting patch-work pieces or appliqués.

Triangle square. A pieced square composed of two triangles; also called "half-square triangle unit."

Value. The lightness or darkness of a color.

Zigzag set. A block arrangement where the blocks are set on point, arranged in vertical rows with large and small setting triangles to give the appearance of zigzag streaks running between the rows.

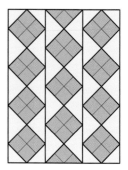

About the Author

Candace Eisner Strick has pursued music, knitting, and sewing her entire life. She divides her time between teaching cello and designing, teaching, and writing about knitting and quiltmaking. She is the author of three knitting books; *The Quilter's Quick Reference Guide* is her first quilting book.

While growing up, Candace sewed her own clothes. With her love of color and geometry that she explores in knitwear, it was only natural that she began to gravitate toward quiltmaking. She started to quilt in the 1970s, but really began to produce quilts 15 years later, when her children were almost grown and she had more time to devote to the craft. Almost entirely self-taught, Candace figured out quilting methods and techniques through hands-on experience. Her favorite quilting technique is now appliqué.

Candace and her husband run Strickwear.com from their home in rural Connecticut.

INDEX